Gospel Light's

BIG BOOK

OF BIBLE FACTS AND FUN

Cool Stuff About the Bible!

- Bible people and events
- Maps and time lines
- Bible book cards, puzzles, coloring pages and more!

Reproducible!

Gospel Light

HOW TO MAKE CLEAN COPIES FROM THIS BOOK

You may make copies of portions of this book with a clean conscience if

However, it is ILLEGAL for you to make copies if

- you (or someone in your organization) are the original purchaser;

- you are using the copies you make for a non-commercial purpose (such as teaching or promoting your ministry) within your church or organization;

- you follow the instructions provided in this book.

- you are using the material to promote, advertise or sell a product or service other than for ministry fund-raising;

- you are using the material in or on a product for sale; or

- you or your organization are not the original purchaser of this book.

By following these guidelines you help us keep our products affordable.
Thank you,
Gospel Light

Editorial Staff

Founder, Dr. Henrietta Mears • **Publisher Emeritus,** William T. Greig • **Publisher, Children's Curriculum and Resources,** Bill Greig III • **Senior Consulting Publisher,** Dr. Elmer L. Towns • **Product Line Manager,** Cary Maxon • **Senior Managing Editor,** Sheryl Haystead • **Senior Consulting Editor,** Wesley Haystead, M.S.Ed. • **Senior Editor, Biblical and Theological Issues,** Bayard Taylor, M.Div. • **Editor,** Mary Davis • **Contributing Editors,** Janis Halverson, Jonelle Stevens • **Art Directors,** Lenndy McCullough, Christina Renée Sharp, Samantha A. Hsu • **Designer,** Zelle Olson

CONTENTS

Matthew 5:3-9

"Blessed are the poor in spirit, for theirs is the kingdom of heaven. Blessed are those who mourn, for they will be comforted. Blessed are the meek, for they will inherit the earth. Blessed are those who hunger and thirst for righteousness, for they will be filled. Blessed are the merciful, for they will be shown mercy. Blessed are the pure in heart, for they will see God. Blessed are the peacemakers, for they will be called sons of God."

HOW TO USE THIS BOOK

if you are the children's pastor,

1 Read "Earth's Most Amazing Book" (p. 7) and "The Value of Good Bible Skills" (p. 8) to get an understanding of the purpose and goals of *The Big Book of Bible Facts and Fun*.

2 Look at the Contents and then skim through this book to get an idea of the kinds of resources that are provided.

3 At the beginning of each teaching term, refer to the scope and sequence of the curriculum being used in your children's program and use the Contents and the Index to locate resources in this book that will enrich students' understanding of the lessons. Photocopy the needed pages and provide them to teachers and small-group leaders at least one week prior to the lesson.

4 Consider providing a copy of *The Big Book of Bible Facts and Fun* for each classroom for students to use as a general Bible study resource.

"Find out how to help kids deepen their understanding of Earth's Most Amazing Book!"

if you are a teacher or small-group leader in any children's program (Sunday School, second hour, mid-week, etc.),

1 Read "Earth's Most Amazing Book" (p. 7) and "The Value of Good Bible Skills" (p. 8) to get an understanding of the purpose and goals of *The Big Book of Bible Facts and Fun*.

2 Look at the Contents and then skim through this book to get an idea of the kinds of resources that are provided.

3 As you prepare a lesson for the program in which you serve, use the Contents and the Index to choose resources (information sheets, puzzles, maps, etc.) in this book that will enrich your students' understanding of the lesson. Photocopy needed pages ahead of time.

INTRODUCTION: EARTH'S MOST AMAZING BOOK

The Bible is one book, one history, one story—His story. The Bible is also a library, a collection of diverse kinds of writing. Behind billions of events stands God, the builder of history, the maker of the ages. Eternity bounds the one side, eternity bounds the other side, and time is in between. From the origins described in Genesis to the endings in Revelation, God is working things out. Go down into the minutest detail everywhere and see that there is one great purpose moving through the ages: the eternal design of the Almighty God to redeem a wrecked and ruined world.

Many people know the Bible characters and the principal events but are hopelessly lost when they are called upon to connect the stories in a meaningful order. The Bible is one book, and you cannot read it only in bits and pieces and expect to comprehend the magnificence of divine revelation. You must see it in its completeness. God has taken pains to progressively reveal Himself and His plan, and we should take pains to read it from beginning to end. Don't suppose reading little scraps can compensate for doing deep and consecutive work on the Bible itself. One would scorn to read any other book, even the lightest novel, in the haphazard fashion in which many read the Bible.

Pick up the "pearls" in the Scriptures and string them into order from Genesis to Revelation so that you can think through the Bible story. Give the Book a chance to speak for itself, to make its own impression and to bear its own testimony. You will find a unity of thought that indicates that one mind inspired the writing of the whole series of books; it bears on its face the stamp of its Author, showing that in every sense, it is the Word of God.

The whole Bible is built around the story of Christ and His promise of life everlasting to all people. The Old Testament is the account of a nation (God's people, the Jewish nation); the New Testament is an account of a Man (who called Himself the Son of man). The nation was founded and nurtured by God in order to bring the Man into the world. His appearance on the earth is the central event of all history. The Old Testament sets the stage for this event; the New Testament describes it.

As a man, Jesus Christ lived the most perfect life ever known. He was kind, tender, gentle, patient and sympathetic. He loved people. He worked marvelous miracles to feed the hungry. Multitudes—weary, pain-ridden and heartsick—came to Him, and He gave them rest. He died to take away the sin of the world and to become the Savior of all people.

Then He rose from the dead. He is alive today. He is not merely a historical character but also a living person—the most important person in history and the One whose vital force transforms the world today! And He promises eternal life to all who come to Him.

The writers of the epistles tell us the kind of life we should live because of Christ's work for us. The secret of Christian living is simply to allow Christ to meet our needs. There is nothing mysterious about faith. It is a simple act of will. Either we will believe God or we won't. We decide. When we decide to believe God absolutely, supernatural life and power enter our lives. A miracle is wrought within us, and the story of God's goodness continues in our lives.

Adapted from *What the Bible Is All About* by Henrietta C. Mears.

THE VALUE OF GOOD BIBLE SKILLS

Imagine sitting down at a computer, staring at a blank screen, knowing that all the information you need is right at your fingertips—but not knowing how to access it. When children are told that what they need is in the Bible, yet don't know how to access the information, they must feel similarly frustrated! We drill children to memorize their names, addresses and phone numbers, but too often we don't take responsibility for teaching them how to get where they need to go in God's Word.

God's long-range goal for every child is to "reach unity in the faith and in the knowledge of the Son of God and become mature, attaining to the whole measure of the fullness of Christ" (Ephesians 4:13). Teaching students how to use the Bible *equips* them to grow and mature.

The beginning of this great process occurs as loving Christian adults work patiently, introducing God's Word through a variety of learning experiences that connect with each

student's level of development and understanding. *The Big Book of Bible Facts and Fun* approaches the Bible in ways that will engage kids in opening their Bibles, finding out more about what they don't understand and discover new ways to study Scripture. The ultimate goal is to gain understanding, which in turn will result in a desire for an ever-deepening relationship with God. Good Bible skills provide a foundation that will serve a person well throughout that growing relationship.

A final word: Few things more effectively communicate the power of God's Word to your students than your own attitudes and actions! Kids sense that the Bible is true and significant when the adults around them use it, respect it and get excited about what God does through His Word. Communicate eagerly the ways in which God's Word helps you in daily life as you help them to gain skills or learn information that help them use the Bible for themselves—it *is* Earth's Most Amazing Book!

Many adult Christians look back to their elementary years as the time when they accepted Christ as Savior. Elementary-age students are not only able to understand their own personal need of forgiveness, but they are also interested in Jesus' death and resurrection as the means by which God provides salvation. In addition, children at this age are capable of growing in their faith through prayer, Bible reading, worship and service.

However, these youngsters are still limited in their understanding and immature in following through on their intentions and commitments. So they need thoughtful, patient guidance in coming to know Christ personally and continuing to grow in Him. Here are steps to leading a child to Christ.

1. Pray.

Ask God to prepare the students in your group to receive the good news about Jesus and to prepare you to effectively communicate with them.

2. Present the good news.

Use words and phrases that students understand. The following outline seeks to avoid symbolism that will confuse these literal-minded thinkers. *Discuss these points slowly enough* to allow time for thinking and comprehending.

a. God wants you to become His child. Do you know why God wants you in His family? (See 1 John 3:1.)

b. You and all the people in the world have done wrong things and disobeyed God. The Bible word for doing wrong is "sin." What do you think should happen to us when we sin? (See Romans 3:23; 6:23.)

c. God loves you so much, He sent His Son to die on the cross for your sin. Because Jesus never sinned, He is the only one who can take the punishment for your sin. (See 1 Corinthians 15:3; 1 John 4:14.)

d. Are you sorry for your sin? Tell God that you are. Do you believe Jesus died to take the punishment for your sin and is alive today? If you tell God you are sorry for your sin and tell Him you do believe and accept Jesus' death to take away your sin—God forgives all your sin. (See 1 John 1:9.)

e. The Bible says that when you believe that Jesus is God's Son and that He is alive today, you receive God's gift of eternal life. This gift makes you a child of God. This means God is with you now and forever. (See John 3:16.)

Give students many opportunities to think about what it means to be a Christian. Expose them to a variety of lessons and descriptions of the meaning of salvation to increase their understanding.

3. Talk individually with students.

Talking about salvation one-on-one creates opportunities to ask and answer questions. Ask questions that move the student beyond simple yes-or-no answers or recitation of memorized information. Ask open-ended, "what do you think?" questions such as:

• Why do you think it's important to . . . ?

• What are some things you really like about Jesus?

• Why do you think that Jesus had to die in order for people to be forgiven?

• What difference do you think it makes for a person to be forgiven?

Answers to these open-ended questions will help you discern how much the student does or does not understand.

4. Offer opportunities without pressure.

Any child is vulnerable to being manipulated by adults. A good way to guard against coercing a student's response is to simply pause periodically and ask, "Would you like to hear more about this now or at another time?" Loving acceptance of the student, even when he or she is not fully interested in pursuing the matter, is crucial in building and maintaining positive attitudes toward becoming part of God's family.

5. Give time to think and pray.

There is great value in encouraging a student to think and pray about what you have said before making a response. Also allow moments for quiet thinking about questions you ask.

6. Respect the student's response.

Whether or not a student declares faith in Jesus Christ, there is a need for adults to accept the student's action. There is also a need to realize that a student's initial responses to Jesus are just the beginning of a lifelong process of growing in faith.

7. Guide the student in further growth.

Here are three important parts in the nurturing process:

a. *Talk regularly about your relationship with God.* As you talk about your relationship, the student will begin to feel that it's OK to talk about such things. Then you can comfortably ask the student to share his or her thoughts and feelings, and encourage the student to ask questions of you.

b. *Prepare the student to deal with doubts.* Emphasize that certainty about salvation is not dependent on our feelings or doing enough good deeds. Show the student places in God's Word that clearly declare that salvation comes by grace through faith (e.g., John 1:12; Ephesians 2:8-9; Hebrews 11:6; 1 John 5:11).

c. *Teach the student to confess all sin.* To confess means to admit or to agree. Confessing sins means agreeing with God that we really have sinned. Assure the student that confession always results in forgiveness. (See 1 John 1:9.)

EARTH'S MOST AMAZING BOOK: A QUICK TOUR

When starting an adventure, it's a good idea to look ahead before you start exploring. So, get ready to

❋ investigate the creation of the universe!

❋ check out narrow escapes and courageous showdowns!

❋ hunt down heroes, villains and ordinary folk!

Amazing!

All that (and more!) happens in the **Old Testament** part of the Bible.

Then, with the flip of a few pages, you will

❋ meet evil kings and powerful leaders!

❋ discover an angel who opens prison doors!

❋ find the Person who will make your whole life different!

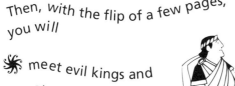

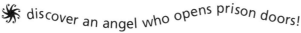

Now we're talking about the **New Testament** part of the Bible.

All the stories in the Bible—from Adam and Eve to the very end—fit together to show us God's great plan for our world and for our own lives. That's an **adventure** you won't want to miss!

BUT WAIT! THERE'S MORE!

⟶

IT'S A MESSAGE!
IT'S A STORY!
IT'S A LIBRARY!
IT'S—THE BIBLE!

It's a Message!

Over many hundreds of years God used many different writers to produce this book. The writers were different ages and had different backgrounds, but what they all wrote carried the same wonderful **message**—

The Savior will come!

Old Testament

The Savior has come!

New Testament

What are some names you have heard people call the Bible? Do you know what those names mean?

+ Bible (book)
+ God's Word (God's truth)
+ The Gospel (good news)

+ Scripture (writings)
+ Holy Bible (special book)
+ The Law (God's rules)

The word "Bible" is from the Greek word that simply means "book," but the Bible is no ordinary book. That's why most Bibles have the word "Holy" ("special or chosen by God") in the title.

IT'S A STORY!

The Bible tells us what God wants us to know about Himself and His plan for us. This exciting, true story is God's **story.**

THE BIG PICTURE OF THE BIBLE

Old Testament   New Testament

Creation   Jesus promised JESUS! Great things that happened Us
        to come   because of Jesus

it's a Library!

When you hold a Bible in your hands and thumb through its pages (or check out the contents page in the front), you see that the Bible is a collection of 66 books—a **library**!

A Library with Two Sections

There are 39 books in the first section. This section makes up about three-fourths of the whole library. It's called the **Old Testament**.

There are 27 books in the second section. This part makes up the last fourth of the library. It's called the **New Testament.**

A Library That's Easy to Use

Besides having only two parts, this library of books in the Bible is easy to use.

So that you can quickly find your way around, nearly all of the books are divided into chapters; and all of the chapters are divided into verses.

To find something in the Bible, all you have to do is look up its **reference**— just like you look up an address! For example, the reference Genesis 1:1 means look in the book of Genesis, chapter 1, verse 1. It's that easy!

PART ONE: OLD TESTAMENT

Think **promise**—the word "testament" means a promise. The entire **Old Testament** is the story of the parts of a wonderful **promise** God made! There are five sections in the Old Testament and that **promise** is found in every section!

SECTION 1:
The first **five** books are called the books of the **Law**. These books tell about the creation of the world and how God chose a family that grew into a nation—Israel—to help fulfill His **promise**. It tells how God freed Israel from slavery, cared for them through 40 years in a desert and gave them His laws. (That didn't mean they always obeyed!)

Right from the start, people disobeyed Him, causing one problem after another. But also right from the start, God **promised** a way **to make things right** again.

SECTION 2:
The next **12** books are called the books of **History.** They tell the story of God's nation, Israel, and start at the time the Israelites entered the land God had promised.

When the Israelites obeyed Him, God defeated their enemies. But **more** often, God's people **disobeyed** and got in serious trouble! There were a few kings and queens who did right—and many who didn't! The disobedience led to fighting; the fighting led to Israel splitting in two, and both halves ended up **cap-**

tured by enemies who sent many away to foreign lands. The books of History **end** at the time some of those people **returned** to the land of Israel.

SECTION 3:

In the very middle of the Bible are **five** books called **Poetry.** These poems and songs were written by many different people—including David king of Israel and his son Solomon. This **poetry** describes the

greatness of God and the beauty of His creation, gives wise **advice** and **answers** many hard questions. The books of Poetry also give **more promises of the great leader** God would send His people!

SECTIONS 4 & 5:

During the years we read about in the books of History, God sent many messengers, called **prophets,** to His people. These prophets spoke or wrote what God wanted His people to know. They gave many **warn-**

ings to obey God and many **more promises** about the **great King and Savior who was coming!**

The first five books of prophecy are called the "Major Prophets" because these books are longer than the "Minor Prophets," 12 smaller books that complete the Old Testament.

PART TWO: NEW TESTAMENT

The New Testament tells about **how** God's promise came **true** and how God's keeping of His promise **changes everything!**

The word "gospel" means "good news." The **four Gospels** tell the **good news**: The King and Savior God had **promised** really did come!

They tell about **Jesus'** birth, life and teachings—and how **many** of God's promises came **true** when Jesus died on the cross to take the punishment for our sins. **More** of God's **promises** came true when Jesus came back to life!

The **Acts of the Apostles** tells what God's **Holy Spirit** did through people who took the **good news** about Jesus to the rest of the world! It tells how Peter, Philip and then Paul spread the **good news**, sharing God's **promise** with everyone—and causing such a stir that people said they were **turning the world upside down!**

The Bible ends with **Letters. Thirteen** are from **Paul**— most written to **churches** and a few written to

people Paul knew. These letters **encouraged** and **taught** those people more about Jesus. Those letters still **teach us** how God's **promise** changes our lives!

Eight letters were written by other **leaders** in the **Early Church** and were sent from **church to church.**

The **last book** of the Bible is a **letter**, too. It's addressed to **seven churches.** It tells of a **prophecy** (or revelation) given to John about the **future.** A lot of this book may be hard to understand, but the great big **promise** here is clear: **Jesus** will come back to Earth, and **everyone** will know He really is the **King of kings** and **Lord of lords**!

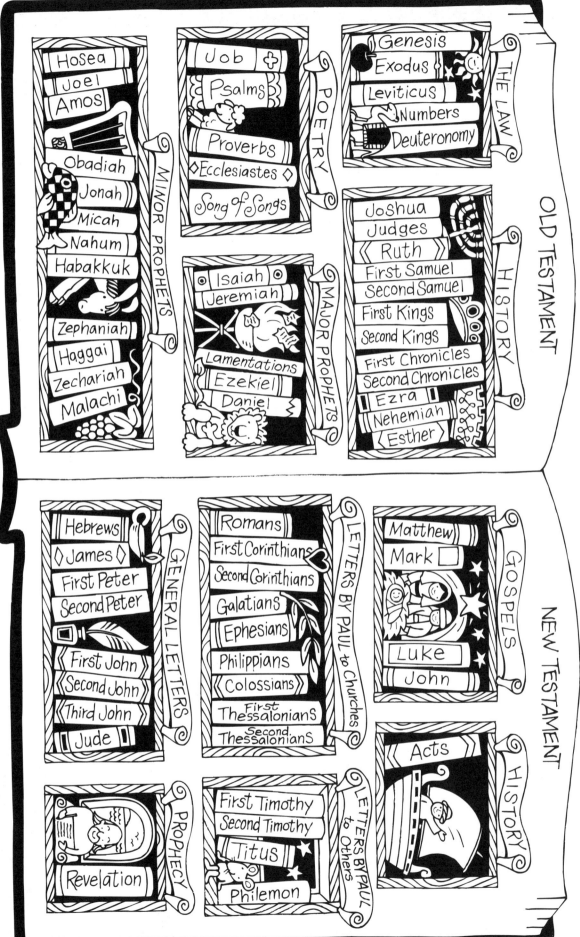

THE BIBLE—A LIBRARY OF SMALLER BOOKS

THE LANGUAGES OF THE BIBLE

When God first gave His word to the people who wrote it down, it wasn't called the Bible. It wasn't even a book! God's words were written on scrolls by people who lived in different places, over thousands of years. The words in the scrolls were not written in English, either. They were written mainly in two languages, Hebrew and Greek.

Hebrew

The scrolls that became the Old Testament (the part of God's Word written before Jesus was born) were written mostly in Hebrew. Hebrew is the language that the people of Israel spoke. Hebrew is still spoken and written in Israel! It is also spoken and written by many people around the world.

The Hebrew alphabet looks quite different from English. First, the letters in Hebrew words are written from *right* to *left* (we read English left to right). That means that when you read a book written in Hebrew, you begin at what we might think is the *back* of the book! Hebrew has no vowels (like the English *a, e, i, o* and *u*). Instead, Hebrew words sometimes have small marks near the letters to show how the word is pronounced.

These are the first letters in the Hebrew alphabet. The first two letters (remember, right to left!) are called *alef* and *bet*. That's the reason the Hebrew alphabet is often called the *alefbet*. There are 27 letters, one more than we have in English.

Greek

The Roman Empire (where Jesus, the disciples and Paul lived) used Latin as the official language of the government. But the people in the Empire spoke *dozens* of different languages! So Greek had become the common language, one that most people could speak, write and understand. When God gave the words that became the New Testament, the people wrote those scrolls and letters in Greek. Although Latin is not spoken anymore, Greek is still spoken today, both in Greece and around the world.

$$\alpha \ \beta \ \gamma \ \delta \ \epsilon \ \zeta$$

The Greek alphabet looks like this. It has 24 letters. Many words we use today came directly from Greek, such as daughter (Greek *thugatyr*), anchor (Greek *ankyra*) and logic (Greek *logikos*). Medical and scientific words are often created from Greek words (amoeba, archaeology, etc.).

THE DEAD SEA SCROLLS

The words in your copy of the Bible were first written down a long, long time ago. They were written by men through whom God chose to speak. We don't have the first copies of the books of the Bible. But other people who knew how important God's Word is made some extra copies.

God watched over this copying of His Word. As the years passed and the old copies got lost or hard to read, new copies were made. Some of the new copies were made in other languages so everyone could understand God's Word.

If you have ever tried to copy something word for word, you know that it is hard to do it correctly; usually there are some mistakes. People began to worry that, over the years, some mistakes might have been made in copying God's Word.

But in the 1940s, a discovery was made that proved that those who copied the Bible had been very, very careful. A shepherd boy in the Bible lands found a cave that had been forgotten for a long time. The cave was near the Dead Sea. Inside the cave the boy found scrolls that had been hidden in jars. These scrolls contained several books of the Bible. They had been copied by people who lived when Jesus lived on Earth!

People who knew a lot about what is written in the Bible checked the Bible we have today with this very old copy. They found that God had truly protected His Word. We can know for sure that what we read in our Bible is the same message God gave to the first writers.

BIBLE BOOK CARDS

Provide these cards to help students:

• learn the names of the books of the Bible.

• practice ordering the books of the Bible.

• recall the main content of each book.

How to Prepare

1. Photocopy pages onto card stock or heavy paper.

2. Invite volunteers to color cards with fine-tip markers, if desired.

3. Laminate or cover pages with clear Con-Tact paper.

4. Cut cards apart along dark lines with scissors or a paper cutter.

5. Bundle cards into sets with rubber bands; store sets in resealable plastic bags.

Tips

Involve students in preparing cards (coloring, cutting) to increase their interest.

Prepare several sets for classroom use; consider preparing individual sets for each student to color and take home for personal review of Bible books.

Games

1. Play a game like Go Fish. The goal is to collect four cards in correct order.

2. Order, Order! Distribute two cards to every player. Players move around the room until your signal, when they quickly move to stand and display cards in correct Bible order.

3. Lay 12 to 16 identical cards from two sets facedown. Play a game like Concentration: Players take turns to flip 2 cards to find matching pairs; pairs are kept by each player. Count pairs to determine the winner.

4. Play a game like War: Players shuffle and divide a set of cards between them, and then simultaneously turn over top cards from their piles, reading book names aloud. Player whose card comes later in the Bible collects both cards. Once all cards are played, players work together to correctly order all cards.

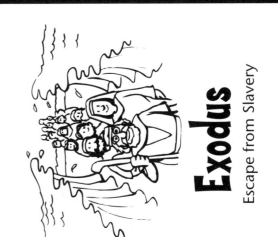

Leviticus
God's Plan for Worship

LAW

2 Samuel
David the King

HISTORY

Numbers
Wandering in the Desert

LAW

1 Samuel
The Last Judge; the First King

HISTORY

Deuteronomy
Reminders of the Law

LAW

Ruth
True Loyalty

HISTORY

Joshua
Into the Promised Land

HISTORY

Judges
Leaders of God's People

HISTORY

1 Kings
The Kingdom Divides

JUDAH
ISRAEL

HISTORY

Job
When Trouble Comes

POETRY

2 Kings
Kings and Prophets

HISTORY

Esther
A Queen's Bravery

HISTORY

1 Chronicles
David's Kingdom

HISTORY

Nehemiah
Rebuilding the Walls

HISTORY

2 Chronicles
Solomon and the Kings of Judah

Ezra
Return to Jerusalem

HISTORY

Psalms

Poems, Prayers and Songs

POETRY

Ezekiel

Strengthened by God

MAJOR PROPHETS

Proverbs

A Word to the Wise

POETRY

Lamentations

Prayers of Sadness

MAJOR PROPHETS

Ecclesiastes

The True Source of Wisdom

POETRY

Jeremiah

God's Future for Israel

MAJOR PROPHETS

Song of Songs

Royal Love Songs

POETRY

To us a child is born.

Isaiah

God's Plan for Salvation

MAJOR PROPHETS

Nahum

God's Justice and Love

Daniel

Courage to Obey

Micah

Judgment and Hope

The Lord has a case against His people.

Hosea

A Picture of God's Love

Jonah

God's Mercy to All People

Joel

Past Failures and Future Promises

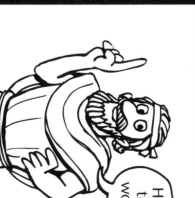

Obadiah

Israel Will Triumph

Amos

Warnings Against Sin

Hear this word...

Luke

Jesus the Son of Man

 GOSPELS

Habakkuk

A Conversation with God

 MINOR PROPHETS

Mark

Jesus the Servant

 GOSPELS

Zephaniah

Sorrow and Singing

 MINOR PROPHETS

Matthew

Jesus the King

GOSPELS

Haggai

Return and Rebuild

MINOR PROPHETS

The Lord you are seeking will come.

Malachi

Trust God for the Coming Savior

 MINOR PROPHETS

Your king is coming to you.

Zechariah

Prepare for the King

MINOR PROPHETS

John
Jesus the Son of God

 GOSPELS

Philippians
Follow Jesus in Everything

LETTERS

Acts
God's Family Grows

HISTORY

Ephesians
New Life in Christ

LETTERS

Romans
God's Amazing Grace

LETTERS

Galatians
Trust Only in Jesus

LETTERS

1 Corinthians
Living as Christians

LETTERS

2 Corinthians
Stay Away from False Teachers

LETTERS

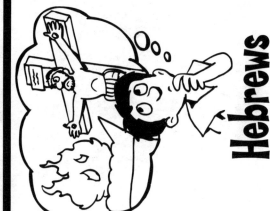

Hebrews

Jesus the Greatest Priest

Colossians

Christ in Charge

Philemon

A Servant Forgiven

Jesus is our hope.

1 Thessalonians

Jesus Our Hope

Titus

Encouragement for God's Leaders

2 Thessalonians

Jesus Will Return

2 Timothy

Stand Against Persecution

1 Timothy

Advice for Young Leaders

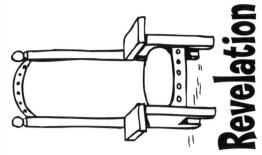

Revelation
The Return of the King

PROPHECY

James
Live Your Faith

LETTERS

Jude
Teach the Truth

LETTERS

1 Peter
Look to Jesus for Help

LETTERS

3 John
Be Faithful

LETTERS

2 Peter
All We Need in Jesus

LETTERS

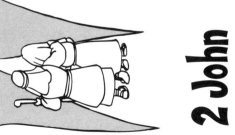

2 John
Follow Only God

LETTERS

1 John
Loved by God

LETTERS

THE BIBLE
Cookie Search

Cross out all the even-numbered cookies. Then write on the blank lines the words in the odd-numbered cookies in order beginning with 1,3,5, etc. You will find out why it s important to read and study God s Word.

15 heart	**16** some	**11** in	**27** against	**12** love
9 word	**6** my	**20** Lord	**3** have	**18** wrong
21 might	**19** I	**17** that	**4** all	**13** my
25 sin	**84** soul	**2** God	**5** hidden	**10** sad
7 your	**23** not	**1** I	**8** good	**29** you

_____

_____

_____

_____. Psalm 119:11

What Do You Know?

Circle the letter under the **T** if the sentence is true. Circle the letter under the **F** if the sentence if false. You will need to use your Bible to find some of the answers.

	T	F
1.	S	S
2.	C	C
3.	R	R
4.	I	I
5.	P	B
6.	T	E
7.	S	U
8.	R	C
9.	E	O
10.	M	P
11.	E	I
12.	A	E
13.	D	N
14.	G	S
15.	W	O
16.	R	D
17.	I	S
18.	T	L
19.	I	A
20.	W	N
21.	G	S

1. There are 27 Gospels.
2. There are 39 Old Testament books.
3. The book of Romans was written by Paul (see Romans 1:1).
4. The book of Titus was written by Titus (see Titus 1:1,4).
5. Acts tells what the followers of Jesus did to teach others about Him.
6. There are 150 Psalms (poems or songs which praise God).
7. The book of Amos comes after the book of Jonah.
8. There are three sets of books which have the same name in the Old Testament and five sets in the New Testament.
9. Leviticus 19:11 could help you decide whether or not to tell the truth.
10. Philemon comes after Titus.
11. Ezekiel comes before Daniel.
12. 1 John 4:9 tells about God's love for us.
13. Genesis is the first book of the New Testament.
14. The book of Jonah is in the New Testament.
15. Matthew, Mark, Luke and John all tell the stories of Jesus' life.
16. Malachi is the last book of the Old Testament.
17. 1 Corinthians has more chapters than 2 Corinthians.
18. The book which talks about someone being thrown in a lions' den is called Daniel.
19. The book of Exodus talks about the Israelites exiting, or leaving, Egypt.
20. The book of Revelation is in the Old Testament.
21. There are four books in the New Testament which have the word "John" in their name.

(Another name for the Bible is "Holy Scripture.")

Write the circled letters in order in the numbered boxes to find an important definition.

Write the uncircled letters in order in these numbered boxes to find out who copied the Scriptures onto scrolls.

BIBLE BOOKS
Bible Book Basics

Draw an arrow in the box to show which way you have to go in your Bible to move from the first book listed to the second book listed.

FROM   TO

Psalms [ ] Leviticus

Mark [ ] John

1 Corinthians [ ] Ephesians

Romans [ ] 1 Thessalonians

Jeremiah [ ] Micah

Haggai [ ] 1 Kings

Ezekiel [ ] Acts

Use your Bible to fill in the correct answers.

The book

before Ecclesiastes _____

after Joshua _____

before Jude _____

after Ezra _____

before Micah _____

after Luke _____

before 1 Peter _____

after Job _____

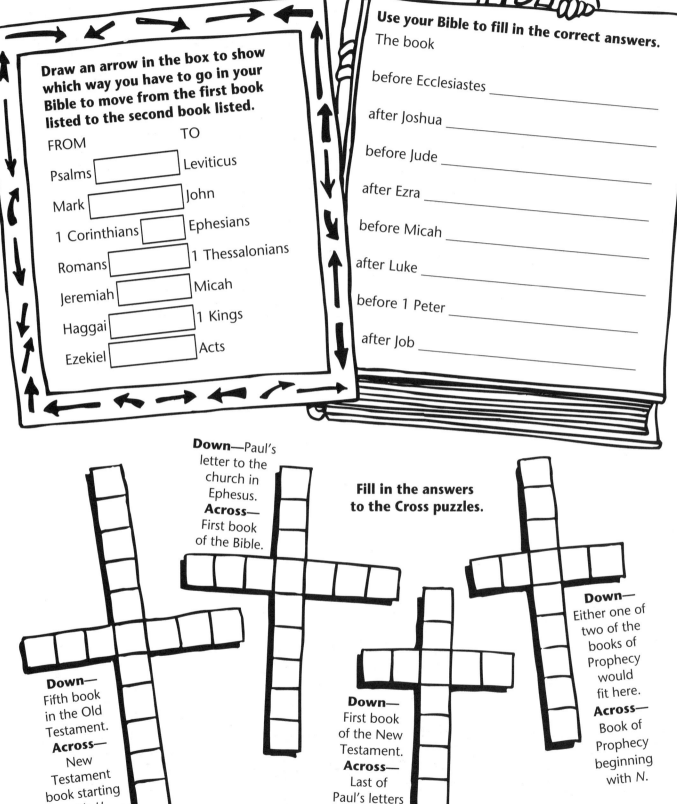

Fill in the answers to the Cross puzzles.

Down—Paul's letter to the church in Ephesus.
Across—First book of the Bible.

Down—Fifth book in the Old Testament.
Across—New Testament book starting with *H*.

Down—First book of the New Testament.
Across—Last of Paul's letters beginning with the letter *T*.

Down—Either one of two of the books of Prophecy would fit here.
Across—Book of Prophecy beginning with *N*.

BIBLE BOOKS

Follow the Clues

1. It is not in any of the books which are laying flat.
2. It is to the left of Romans.
3. It is not a book which has the same name as another book.
4. It has more than four letters in its name.
5. It has the same name as something in an address.

One of the books below has a story about a talking animal. Find where the story is by reading the clues below.

Read _____ 22:21-34 for the story about what happened!
(book you discovered)

In one of the books below you can read about two miraculous escapes from prison.

1. It is not any of the books which are stacked in a pile.
2. It is to the right of Exodus.
3. It is not a book with a person's name.
4. It is not an Old Testament book.

Read _____ 12:5-11 and 16:16-40 for the story about who escaped from prison!
(book you discovered)

BIBLE BOOKS
Hidden Word

Color each space which contains the name of a book of the Bible. Then turn the paper until you can read what word the colored spaces spell.

Genesis	Hannah	Ishmael	Exodus	Law	Obed	Leviticus
Numbers	Letters	Naomi	Deuteronomy	Caleb	Prophets	Joshua
Judges	Ruth	1 Samuel	2 Samuel	1 Kings	2 Kings	1 Chronicles
Abraham	Ezariah	Narnia	Madagascar	Ethiopia	Song of Simon	1 Queen
2 Queen	3 Queen	Jacob	Zeborias	Judah	Priest	2 Chronicles
Singing	Poetry	Rebekah	Methuselah	Rabbi	Nathan	Ezra
Nehemiah	Esther	Job	Psalms	Proverbs	Ecclesiastes	Song of Songs
Pharisee	1 David	2 David	Mordecai	Isaac	Carl	Rahab
Isaiah	Jeremiah	Lamentations	Ezekiel	Daniel	Hosea	Joel
Amos	Namon	Rachel	Obadiah	Joseph	Danny	Jonah
Micah	Nahum	Habakkuk	Zephaniah	Haggai	Zechariah	Malachi
Deborah	Edom	Abigail	Reuben	Levi	Bartholomew	History
Matthew	Philip	Peter	Thaddeus	Judas	Mary	Mark
Luke	John	Acts	Romans	1 Corinthians	2 Corinthians	Galatians
Ephesians	Rome	Galapagos	Hannibal	Lyonius	Grecians	Philippians
Balaam	Solomon	Leah	Barnabas	Salonichus	1 Torah	2 Torah
Colossians	1 Thessalonians	2 Thessalonians	1 Timothy	2 Timothy	Titus	Philemon
Hebrews	Saloam	Seth	James	Abel	Andrew	1 Peter
2 Peter	1 John	2 John	3 John	Jude	Revelation	▓

Hint: Look at the contents page of your Bible for help!

Old Testament Surprise

Color in each section that contains a book of the Old Testament. You'll find a picture of someone who is not found anywhere in the Bible.

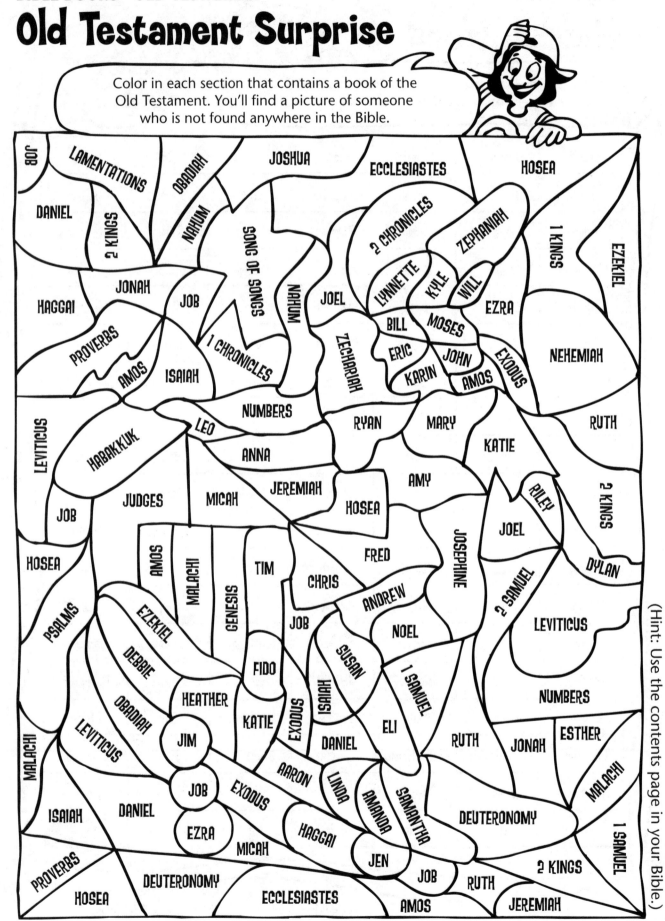

(Hint: Use the contents page in your Bible.)

BIBLE BOOKS—NEW TESTAMENT

Bubble Gum

Follow the lines to move between each gum ball, spelling the names of the New Testament books written on each machine. You may move in any direction.

GOSPELS & HISTORY

Matthew
Mark
Luke
John
Acts

PAUL'S LETTERS

Romans
Corinthians (1,2)
Galatians
Ephesians
Philippians
Colossians
Thessalonians (1,2)
Timothy (1,2)
Titus
Philemon

GENERAL LETTERS & PROPHECY

Hebrews
James
Peter (1,2)
John (1,2,3)
Jude
Revelation

Computer Art

Start at the arrow and draw a line through all the letters that spell the books of the New Testament in order. You may move in any direction. When you are finished, you will see a picture of an animal people used for travel in Bible times.

V	D	B	L	I	N	T	R	B	G	F	D	H	A	B	Q	P	S	T	L	D	A	E	G	R	V	L	T
J	L	O	E	Q	S	T	O	M	V	B	T	S	R	C	K	R	F	O	R	E	U	L	C	J	K	Y	Q
S	T	U	G	I	F	R	E	O	J	Y	C	E	O	M	D	O	L	U	T	J	D	V	O	R	P	X	Z
D	S	B	F	M	I	V	F	Q	T	N	A	W	R	B	A	E	G	Q	P	K	F	R	C	I	N	T	V
C	W	O	D	T	A	O	P	Z	O	H	A	J	S	E	N	S	1	C	Q	U	H	K	2	X	A	I	H
E	Y	K	L	E	U	K	G	E	J	M	J	3	N	H	N	O	M	O	R	H	D	T	S	S	N	O	F
N	J	G	F	I	B	L	U	K	E	H	O	O	I	H	O	J	E	L	I	N	P	A	N	G	Q	L	U
K	F	M	A	W	R	K	1	S	J	N	X	N	T	A	L	2	N	I	H	T	H	I	L	A	K	E	R
V	A	U	C	M	A	P	X	U	D	E	R	E	V	E	1	J	O	H	P	S	U	T	A	F	O	M	W
R	N	L	K	W	E	T	E	R	2	P	E	T	E	R	T	H	Y	T	I	T	A	I	M	W	B	Q	T
U	F	H	E	A	S	1	T	I	M	O	T	2	I	M	O	L	O	C	S	S	N	Q	K	Q	L	M	R
W	S	T	I	N	N	S	S	E	H	T	H	Y	T	S	S	O	P	N	L	E	B	F	U	O	U	C	H
E	D	T	B	O	M	A	J	D	M	1	S	N	A	I	D	K	G	A	K	P	M	A	B	E	L	E	O
K	A	R	F	L	P	L	E	W	L	V	F	Q	B	J	F	Q	C	I	T	H	K	W	A	J	A	H	T
M	F	O	W	A	T	V	O	Q	E	U	I	D	R	T	K	M	U	P	R	E	O	E	M	N	F	K	N
T	L	R	Q	S	F	H	N	C	D	L	V	A	W	O	Q	F	I	P	O	S	B	Z	Q	R	B	P	U
A	W	L	S	I	M	C	I	F	W	E	B	N	D	R	C	W	L	T	D	I	Q	I	E	N	A	D	E
E	J	F	E	C	R	P	A	D	K	T	P	Q	M	A	E	U	I	R	Q	A	F	K	B	J	S	L	A
M	P	I	H	T	2	S	N	C	S	R	N	O	L	Y	N	O	H	P	S	N	P	A	M	S	O	N	F

HINT: USE THE CONTENTS PAGE OF YOUR BIBLE FOR HELP.

Swimming Divisions

POOL RULES:
(2) Find the Old Testament book names written below. Draw a line to match each set of books to its division above.

(1) To discover the names of the Old Testament divisions, follow the arrows and change each letter in the inner tubes to the letter that comes before it in the alphabet. Write the name you find on the line below each inner tube.

ISAIAHJEREMIAHLAMENTATI
ONSEZEKIELDANIELHOSEAJ
OELAMOSOBADIAHJONAHMIC
AHNAHUMHABAKKUKZEPHANI
AHHAGGAIZECHARIAHMALACHI

JOBPSALMSPROVERBSECCLESIASTESSONGOFSONGS

JOSHUAJUDGESRUTHFIRSTS
TSRIFLEUMASDNOCESLEUMA
KINGSSECONDKINGSFIRSTC
INORHCDNOCESSELCINORH
CLESEZRANEHEMIAHESTHER

LEVITICUSNUMBERSDEUTERONOMYGENESISEXODUS

BIBLE DIVISIONS—OLD TESTAMENT LAW AND HISTORY

Walking with the israelites

Choose a number from 1 to 17. Follow the path and look for the sandals with the number you chose. Write the letters in order on the blank line with the same number. Repeat with other numbers until the blank lines are filled.

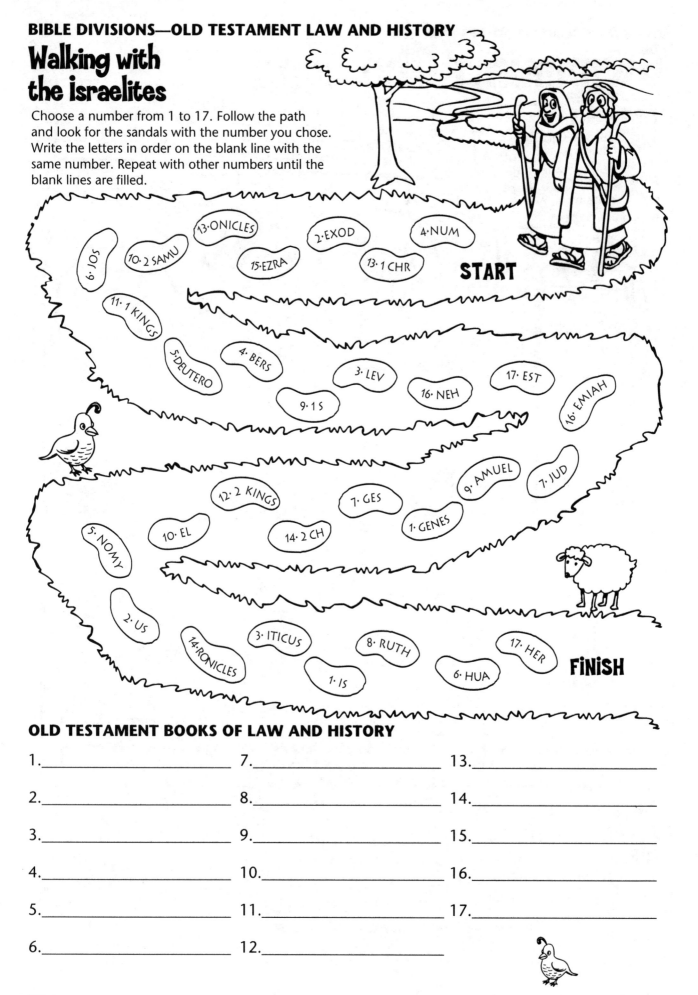

START

FINISH

OLD TESTAMENT BOOKS OF LAW AND HISTORY

1._____   7._____   13._____

2._____   8._____   14._____

3._____   9._____   15._____

4._____   10._____   16._____

5._____   11._____   17._____

6._____   12._____

BIBLE DIVISIONS—OLD TESTAMENT HISTORY
Maze of Scrolls

Collect all the Old Testament books of History in order. There is only one correct path.
(Hint: Use the contents page in your Bible for help.)

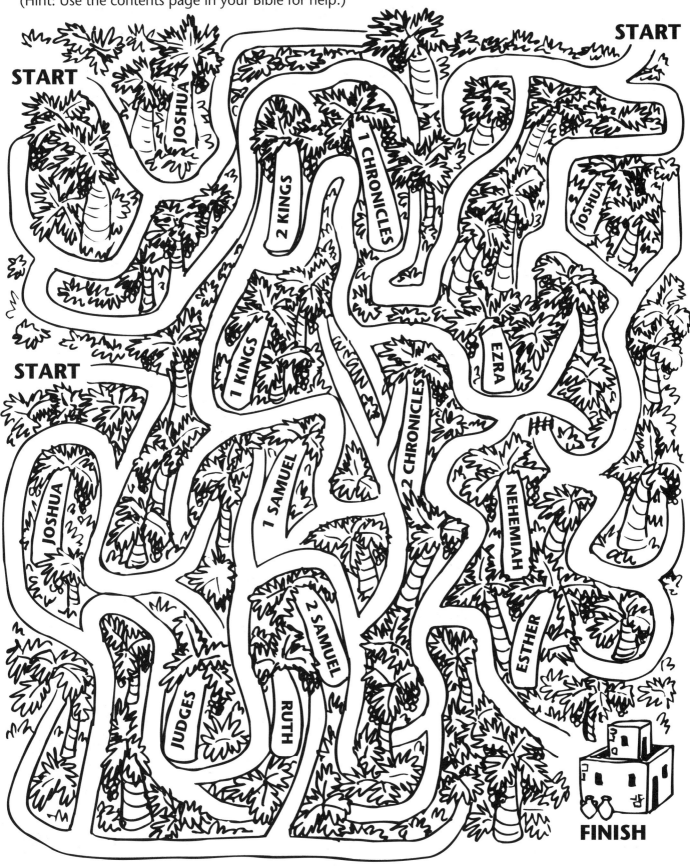

KEY WORD CODE

Decode these books of History. Find the letter in the code line and then discover what it really is by looking directly below the letter in the real line. (For example, the code "SHP" is really the word "CAT.")

Tell your neighbor the other six books of History.

CODE: H I S T O R Y A B C D E F G J K L M N P Q U V W X Z
REAL: A B C D E F G H I J K L M N O P Q R S T U V W X Y Z

1. G O R O F B H R : _____

2. I N H F Q O E : ___I_____

3. C J N R Q H : _____

Use the code to encode these books of History:

1. E Z R R : _____

2. R U T H : _____

3. J U D G E S : _____

Bonus:

Make a new code using the word "Poetry" as the key word. First write the letters of "Poetry" above the first letters of the alphabet. Then write the rest of the letters of the alphabet above the letters of the real alphabet, making sure to leave out the letters you already used in the word "Poetry." Next, try using the code you made to encode the three books of Poetry written below.

Which two books of Poetry are missing?

CODE:
REAL: A B C D E F G H I J K L M N O P Q R S T U V W X Y Z

1. P R O V E R B S : _____

2. P S A L M S : _____

3. E C C L E S I A S T E S : _____

BUILDER BONUS:
What groups of books come before and after the books of Prophecy?
What are the names of the five major books of Prophecy?

Missing Halves

These letters got torn in half! Find the halves of the letters that match. Write all the letters with the same pattern on a blank line. Then unscramble the letters to find the names of the divisions in the New Testament.

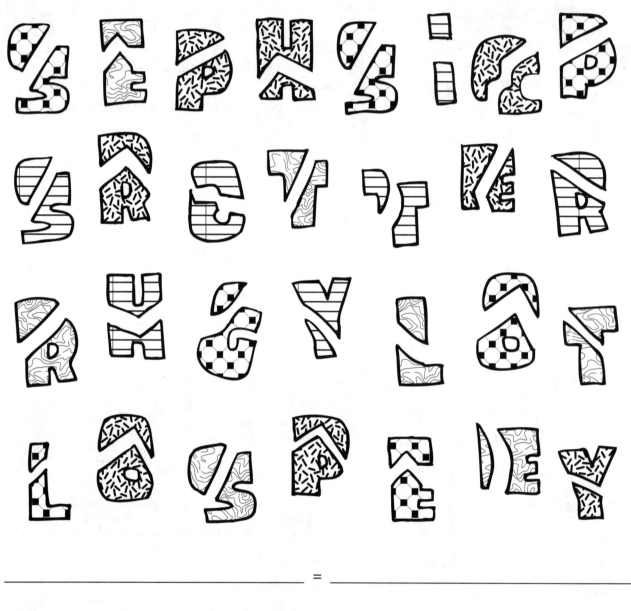

_____ = _____

_____ = _____

_____ = _____

_____ = _____

BIBLE DIVISIONS—NEW TESTAMENT GOSPELS

Balloon Pop

If you follow the directions below, you'll find out what the first division of New Testament books tell us.

Use an *X* to pop all balloons with

1. names of men from the Old Testament;

2. words beginning with S;

3. names of women from the New Testament;

4. names of foods eaten in Bible times.

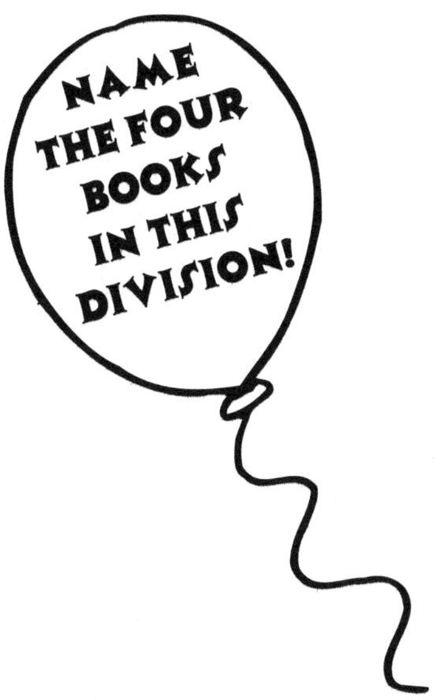

NAME THE FOUR BOOKS IN THIS DIVISION!

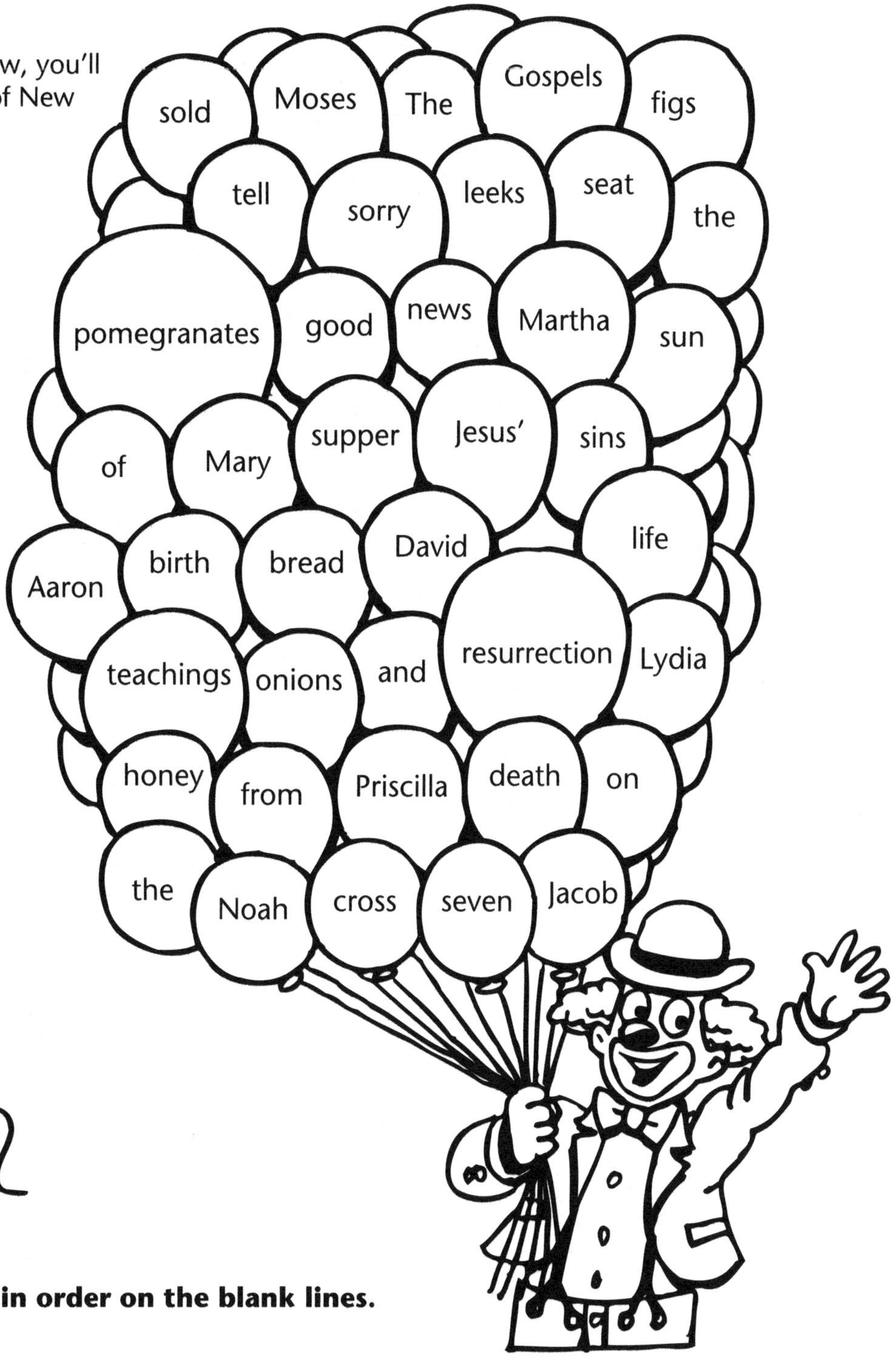

sold   Moses   The   Gospels   figs
tell   sorry   leeks   seat   the
pomegranates   good   news   Martha   sun
of   Mary   supper   Jesus'   sins
Aaron   birth   bread   David   life
teachings   onions   and   resurrection   Lydia
honey   from   Priscilla   death   on
the   Noah   cross   seven   Jacob

Write the remaining words in order on the blank lines.

_____   _____   _____   _____

_____   _____   _____   _____   _____ ,   _____ ,

_____   _____   _____   _____

_____   _____   _____   _____ .

BIBLE DIVISIONS—NEW TESTAMENT LETTERS

Lost Letters

Help the letters get delivered. Collect each letter as you go through the maze.

Ephesians

Romans

Galatians

Philippians

1, 2 Corinthians

START

Colossians

Titus

1, 2 Timothy

Philemon

James

1, 2 Thessalonians

1, 2, 3 John

Hebrews

Jude

1, 2 Peter

THE BIBLE
Cookie Search

Cross out all the even-numbered cookies. Then write on the blank lines the words in the odd-numbered cookies in order beginning with 1,3,5, etc. You will find out why it's important to read and study God's Word.

Row 1: 15 heart | 13 (crossed) time | 11 in | 27 against | 12 (crossed) love
Row 2: 9 word | 2 (crossed) my | 4 (crossed) Lord | 3 have | 8 (crossed) long
Row 3: 21 might | 19 I | 17 that | 24 (crossed) all | 13 my
Row 4: 25 sin | 6 (crossed) soul | 20 (crossed) God | 5 hidden | 10 (crossed) this
Row 5: 7 your | 23 not | 1 I | 8 (crossed) good | 29 you

I have hidden your word in my heart

that I might not sin against you.

Psalm 119:11

THE BIBLE
What Do You Know?

Circle the letter under the **T** if the sentence is true. Circle the letter under the **F** if the sentence if false. You will need to use your Bible to find some of the answers.

1. There are 27 Gospels.
2. There are 39 Old Testament books.
3. The book of Romans was written by Paul (see Romans 1:1).
4. The book of Titus was written by Titus (see Titus 1:1,4).
5. Acts tells what the followers of Jesus did to teach others about Him.
6. There are 150 Psalms (poems or songs which praise God).
7. The book of Amos comes after the book of Jonah.
8. There are three sets of books which have the same name in the Old Testament and five sets in the New Testament.
9. Leviticus 19:11 could help you decide whether or not to tell the truth.
10. Philemon comes after Titus.
11. Ezekiel comes before Daniel.
12. 1 John 4:9 tells about God's love for us.
13. Genesis is the first book of the New Testament.
14. The book of Jonah is in the New Testament.
15. Matthew, Mark, Luke and John all tell the stories of Jesus' life.
16. Malachi is the last book of the Old Testament.
17. 1 Corinthians has more chapters than 2 Corinthians.
18. The book which talks about someone being thrown in a lions' den is called Daniel.
19. The book of Exodus talks about the Israelites exiting, or leaving, Egypt.
20. The book of Revelation is in the Old Testament.
21. There are four books in the New Testament which have the word "John" in their name.

	T	F
1.	S	(S)
2.	(C)	C
3.	(R)	R
4.	R	(I)
5.	(P)	B
6.	(T)	B
7.	S	(U)
8.	(R)	C
9.	(E)	O
10.	(M)	P
11.	(E)	I
12.	(A)	E
13.	A	(N)
14.	G	(S)
15.	(W)	O
16.	(R)	D
17.	(I)	L
18.	(T)	U
19.	(I)	A
20.	W	(N)
21.	(G)	S

Write the circled letters in order in the numbered boxes to find an important definition.

(Another name for the Bible is "Holy Scripture.")

Write the uncircled letters in order in these numbered boxes to find out who copied the Scriptures onto scrolls.

1 2 3 4 5 6 7 8 9: S C R I P T U R E
10 11 12 13 14: M E A N S
15 16 17 18 19 20 21: W R I T I N G

1 2 3 4 5 6 7: S C R I B E S
8 9 10 11 12 13: C O P I E D
14 15 16 17: G O D'S   18 19 20 21: L A W S

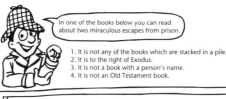

BIBLE BOOKS
Bible Book Basics

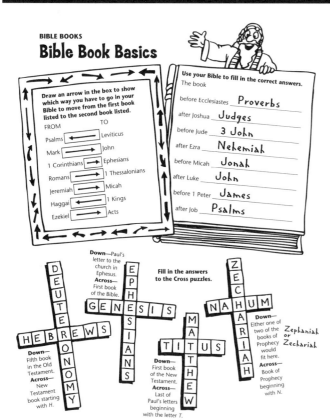

Draw an arrow in the box to show which way you have to go in your Bible to move from the first book listed to the second book listed.

FROM		TO
Psalms	←	Leviticus
Mark	→	John
1 Corinthians	→	Ephesians
Romans	→	1 Thessalonians
Jeremiah	→	Micah
Haggai	←	1 Kings
Ezekiel	→	Acts

Use your Bible to fill in the correct answers.

The book

before Ecclesiastes **Proverbs**

after Joshua **Judges**

before Jude **3 John**

after Ezra **Nehemiah**

before Micah **Jonah**

after Luke **John**

before 1 Peter **James**

after Job **Psalms**

Fill in the answers to the Cross puzzles.

Down—Paul's letter to the church in Ephesus.
Across—First book of the Bible.

Down—Fifth book in the Old Testament.
Across—New Testament book starting with *H*.

Crossword answers: DEUTERONOMY, EPHESIANS, GENESIS, HEBREWS, ZECHARIAH, NAHUM, MATTHEW, TITUS

Down—Either one of two of the books of Prophecy would fit here. *Zephaniah or Zechariah*

Down—First book of the New Testament.
Across—Last of Paul's letters beginning with the letter *T*.

Across—Book of Prophecy beginning with *N*.

BIBLE BOOKS
Follow the Clues

One of the books below has a story about a talking animal. Find where the story is by reading the clues below.

1. It is not in any of the books which are laying flat.
2. It is to the left of Romans.
3. It is not a book which has the same name as another book.
4. It has more than four letters in its name.
5. It has the same name as something in an address.

Books shown: GENESIS, NUMBERS, JOSHUA, 2 KINGS, MARK, ROMANS, 1 CORINTHIANS, 2 CORINTHIANS, REVELATION

Read **Numbers** 22:21-34 for the story about what happened!
(book you discovered)

In one of the books below you can read about two miraculous escapes from prison.

1. It is not any of the books which are stacked in a pile.
2. It is to the right of Exodus.
3. It is not a book with a person's name.
4. It is not an Old Testament book.

Books shown: EXODUS, 1 SAMUEL, 2 SAMUEL, PSALMS, MICAH, ACTS, 1 TIMOTHY, 2 TIMOTHY, 1 PETER, 3 JOHN

Read **Acts** 12:5-11 and 16:16-40 for the story about who escaped from prison!
(book you discovered)

BIBLE BOOKS
Hidden Word

Color each space which contains the name of a book of the Bible. Then turn the paper until you can read what word the colored spaces spell.

Genesis	Hannah	Ishmael	Exodus	Law	Obed	Leviticus
Numbers	Letters	Naomi	Deuteronomy	Caleb	Prophets	Joshua
Judges	Ruth	1 Samuel	2 Samuel	1 Kings	2 Kings	1 Chronicles
Abraham	Ezariah	Narnia	Madagascar	Ethiopia	Song of Simon	1 Queen
2 Queen	3 Queen	Jacob	Zeborias	Judah	Priest	2 Chronicles
Singing	Poetry	Rebekah	Methuselah	Rabbi	Nathan	Ezra
Nehemiah	Esther	Job	Psalms	Proverbs	Ecclesiastes	Song of Songs
Pharisee	1 David	2 David	Mordecai	Isaac	Carl	Rahab
Isaiah	Jeremiah	Lamentations	Ezekiel	Daniel	Hosea	Joel
Amos	Namon	Rachel	Obadiah	Joseph	Danny	Jonah
Micah	Nahum	Habakkuk	Zephaniah	Haggai	Zechariah	Malachi
Deborah	Edom	Abigail	Reuben	Levi	Bartholomew	History
Matthew	Philip	Peter	Thaddeus	Judas	Mary	Mark
Luke	John	Acts	Romans	1 Corinthians	2 Corinthians	Galatians
Ephesians	Rome	Galapagos	Hannibal	Lyonius	Grecians	Philippians
Balaam	Solomon	Leah	Barnabas	Salonichus	1 Torah	2 Torah
Colossians	1 Thessalonians	2 Thessalonians	1 Timothy	2 Timothy	Titus	Philemon
Hebrews	Saloam	Seth	James	Abel	Andrew	1 Peter
2 Peter	1 John	2 John	3 John	Jude	Revelation	

Hint: Look at the contents page of your Bible for help!

BIBLE BOOKS—OLD TESTAMENT
Old Testament Surprise

Color in each section that contains a book of the Old Testament. You'll find a picture of someone who is not found anywhere in the Bible.

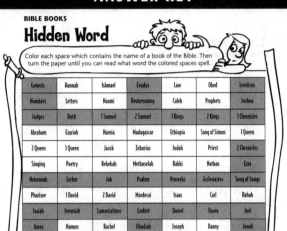

(Hint: Use the contents page in your Bible.)

BIBLE BOOKS—NEW TESTAMENT
Bubble Gum

Follow the lines to move between each gum ball, spelling the names of the New Testament books written on each machine. You may move in any direction.

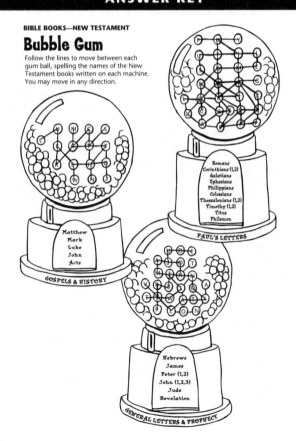

Matthew
Mark
Luke
John
Acts

GOSPELS & HISTORY

Romans
Corinthians (1,2)
Galatians
Ephesians
Philippians
Colossians
Thessalonians (1,2)
Timothy (1,2)
Titus
Philemon

PAUL'S LETTERS

Hebrews
James
Peter (1,2)
John (1,2,3)
Jude
Revelation

GENERAL LETTERS & PROPHECY

BIBLE BOOKS—NEW TESTAMENT
Computer Art

Start at the arrow and draw a line through all the letters that spell the books of the New Testament in order. You may move in any direction. When you are finished, you will see a picture of an animal people used for travel in Bible times.

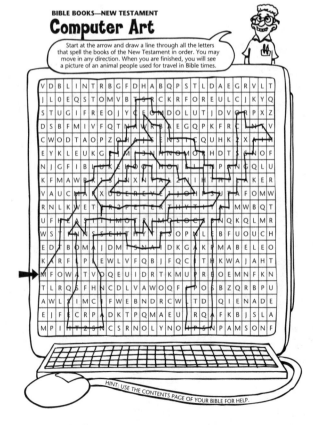

HINT: USE THE CONTENTS PAGE OF YOUR BIBLE FOR HELP.

BIBLE DIVISIONS—OLD TESTAMENT

Swimming Divisions

POOL RULES:
(2) Find the Old Testament book names written below. Draw a line to match each set of books to its division above.

(1) To discover the names of the Old Testament divisions, follow the arrows and change each letter in the inner tubes to the letter that comes before it in the alphabet. Write the name you find on the line below each inner tube.

LAW
HISTORY
POETRY
PROPHECY

JOBPSALMSPROVERBSECCLESIASTESSONGOFSONGS

JOSHUAJUDGESRUTHFIRSTS
TSRIFLEUMASDNOCESLEUMA
KINGSSECONDKINGSFIRSTC
HRONICHDNOCESSELCINORH
CLESEZRANEHEMIAHESTHER

BIBLE DIVISIONS—OLD TESTAMENT LAW AND HISTORY

Walking with the Israelites

Choose a number from 1 to 17. Follow the path and look for the sandals with the number you chose. Write the letters in order on the blank line with the same number. Repeat with other numbers until the blank lines are filled.

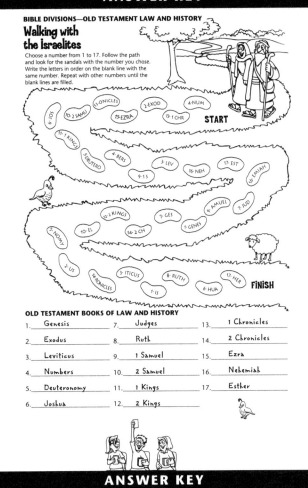

START

FINISH

OLD TESTAMENT BOOKS OF LAW AND HISTORY

1.	Genesis	7.	Judges	13.	1 Chronicles
2.	Exodus	8.	Ruth	14.	2 Chronicles
3.	Leviticus	9.	1 Samuel	15.	Ezra
4.	Numbers	10.	2 Samuel	16.	Nehemiah
5.	Deuteronomy	11.	1 Kings	17.	Esther
6.	Joshua	12.	2 Kings		

BIBLE DIVISIONS—OLD TESTAMENT HISTORY

Maze of Scrolls

Collect all the Old Testament books of History in order. There is only one correct path. (Hint: Use the contents page in your Bible for help.)

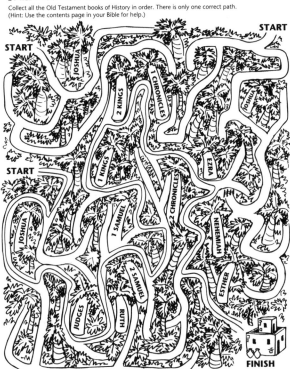

START
START
START
FINISH

BIBLE DIVISIONS—OLD TESTAMENT HISTORY AND POETRY

KEY WORD CODE

Tell your neighbor the other six books of History.

Decode these books of History. Find the letter in the code line and then discover what it really is by looking directly below the letter in the real line. (For example, the code "SHP" is really the word "CAT.")

```
CODE: H I S T O R Y A B C D E F G J K L M N P O U V W X Z
REAL: A B C D E F G H I J K L M N O P Q R S T U V W X Y Z
```

1. GOROFBHA: ___NEHEMIAH___

2. 1 NHFODE: 1 ___SAMUEL___

3. CJNAOH: ___JOSHUA___

Use the code to encode these books of History:

1. EZRA: ___OZMH___

2. RUTH: ___MQPA___

3. JUDGES: ___CQTYON___

Bonus:

Make a new code using the word "Poetry" as the key word. First write the letters of "Poetry" above the first letters of the alphabet. Then write the rest of the letters of the alphabet above the letters of the real alphabet, making sure to leave out the letters you already used in the word "Poetry." Next, try using the code you made to encode the three books of Poetry written below.

Job   Song of Songs

Which two books of Poetry are missing?

```
CODE: P O E T R Y A B C D F G H I J K L M N Q S U V W X Z
REAL: A B C D E F G H I J K L M N O P Q R S T U V W X Y Z
```

1. PROVERBS: ___KMJURMON___

2. PSALMS: ___KNPGHN___

3. ECCLESIASTES: ___REEGRNCPNQRN___

BIBLE DIVISIONS—OLD TESTAMENT PROPHECY

Prophets' Wall

Help the prophets climb up the wall. Write the names of the books of Prophecy in the correct spaces.

Hint: Count the letters in each prophet's name.

BUILDER BONUS:
What groups of books come before and after the books of Prophecy?
What are the names of the five major books of Prophecy?

POETRY
GOSPELS

ISAIAH, JEREMIAH, LAMENTATIONS, EZEKIEL, DANIEL

BIBLE DIVISIONS—NEW TESTAMENT

Missing Halves

These letters got torn in half! Find the halves of the letters that match. Write all the letters with the same pattern on a blank line. Then unscramble the letters to find the names of the divisions in the New Testament.

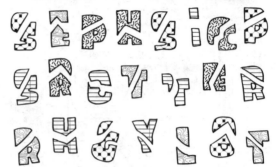

SSPGOLE	=	GOSPELS
ETRLTSE	=	LETTERS
PHCREOPY	=	PROPHECY
ISOTRHY	=	HISTORY

BIBLE DIVISIONS—NEW TESTAMENT GOSPELS

Balloon Pop

If you follow the directions below, you'll find out what the first division of New Testament books tell us.

Use an *X* to pop all balloons with

1. names of men from the Old Testament;
2. words beginning with S;
3. names of women from the New Testament;
4. names of foods eaten in Bible times.

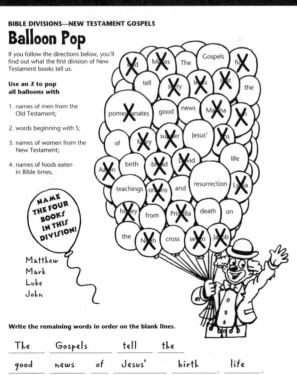

NAME THE FOUR BOOKS IN THIS DIVISION!

Matthew
Mark
Luke
John

Write the remaining words in order on the blank lines.

The	Gospels	tell	the
good	news	of	Jesus'	birth	life
teachings	and	resurrection		from
death	on	the	cross

BIBLE DIVISIONS—NEW TESTAMENT LETTERS

Lost Letters

Help the letters get delivered. Collect each letter as you go through the maze.

How to Use Earth's Most Amazing Book

E. M. A. B.—check it out!

Information pages that help students understand their place in God's family and resource pages to help boost personal Bible study. Section also includes information on how to use Bible study helps, daily Bible reading plans, and a selection of Scripture miniposters (New International Version) to help students learn 10 important Scripture passages.

Joining God's Family

Do you know that the God who made the universe loves you?

He does!

He loves you so much, He wants you to be His child!
God's Word, the Bible, says, "God is love." 1 John 4:8

In the Bible, the word for doing wrong is "sin."
God says that you have sinned and I have sinned.
Our sin keeps us away from God's great love for us.

God's Word says:

"All have sinned and fall short of the glory of God." Romans 3:23

56

But, do you know that you and I, and all the other people in the world, have done wrong things—like forgetting God, and being selfish, and disobeying Him, and hurting others?

We have.

So God sent His Son, Jesus, to show how much He loves you.
Did you know that Jesus took the punishment for your sin?

He did!

Jesus died on the cross so all the wrong things you've done can be forgiven.

God's Word says:

"Christ died for our sins." 1 Corinthians 15:3

Do you know that God is ready to forgive you right now?
He is!
If you admit that you've done wrong things, and if you believe that Jesus died for you and lives today, God will forgive all your sin. God's Word says: "If we confess our sins, he is faithful and just and will forgive us our sins." 1 John 1:9

Do you know that when God forgives you, you become His child?

That's right!

God wants you to be in His family!

God's Word says: "To all who received him, to those who believed in his name, he gave the right to become children of God." John 1:12

Do you know that when you become a part of God's family,
God gives you an awesome gift—eternal life?

He does!

This means Jesus will be with you now and forever!

God's Word says:

"For God so loved the world that he gave his one and only Son,
that whoever believes in him shall not perish but have eternal life." John 3:16

How to ask to be God's child:

You can talk to God in your own words.

1. **Admit that you need to be forgiven.**

2. **Thank God that Jesus died for you.**

3. **Ask God to forgive you and to help you turn away from doing wrong.**

4. **Thank God that Jesus is alive and will be with you forever.**

GROWING IN GOD'S FAMILY

PRO Planner Page!

personal reading organizer

Use this page to create your PRO plan for daily Bible study!

First,
I will thank God for . . .

I will ask God to help me this week to . . .

"Answers to Prayer" Space

Smiley Space

I will set aside
_____ minutes each day to read my Bible. I will draw a smiley face on this page each time I carry out my plan!

BONUS IDEA:
Ask an adult, "What's the best way you have found to study the Bible?"

i will be in
this place to carry out my plan.

I will read each day at _____ o'clock a.m. p.m. (circle one).

(Fill in the time on the clock, too!)

(Draw a picture of the place where you will read.)

HOW TO STUDY THE BIBLE

The Bible (Earth's Most Amazing Book, remember?) is so amazing that there is no end to the ways you can study and learn from it! You will always find something new in the Bible—the official book of God, who invented surprises!

The PCE Method

what I read: Date:

Promises (to trust)	Commands (to obey)	Examples (to follow—or not!)

Note: Not every passage will always have all 3. That's part of the adventure!

The ONE THiNG Method

what i read:

Date:

one thing i already knew:

one thing i did not know:

one insight about God or other people:

one way i can change:

one thing to tell God:

A Plan for Reading Through the Bible

What's so special about reading through the entire Bible? Reading through the whole book is a way to get the big picture of God's plan for history. There are many plans to help people read through the whole Bible. Some help you read through it in a year. But remember, reading through the Bible in a year won't make you a special saint. And you're not a spiritual failure if you don't! It's just a way to get the big picture of God's entire story.

Here are some shorter plans to help you get started (and avoid brain-bruises!):

30 Days of Beginnings

- ☐ Day 1: Genesis 1—2 *How it all began*
- ☐ Day 2: Genesis 3—4 *How it all fell apart*
- ☐ Day 3: Genesis 5—6:4 *Long lives and bad guys*
- ☐ Day 4: Genesis 6:5—7:24 *Earth's driest family*
- ☐ Day 5: Genesis 8—9:19 *The flood ends; promises begin*
- ☐ Day 6: Genesis 11 *From Shem to Abram*
- ☐ Day 7: Genesis 12 *Abram obeys, sort of*
- ☐ Day 8: Genesis 13—14 *Abram and Lot*
- ☐ Day 9: Genesis 15—16 *The promise—not believed*
- ☐ Day 10: Genesis 17—18:15 *The promise—HA!*
- ☐ Day 11: Genesis 18:16—19:29 *Lot escapes Sodom*
- ☐ Day 12: Genesis 21 *Promise kept and other surprises*
- ☐ Day 13: Genesis 22 *Abraham's test and Isaac's cousins*
- ☐ Day 14: Genesis 23—24 *A funeral and a wedding*

- ☐ Day 15: Genesis 25:19-34 *Isaac's twins*
- ☐ Day 16: Genesis 27—28:9 *Jacob sneaks and runs*
- ☐ Day 17: Genesis 29 *Jacob falls in love*
- ☐ Day 18: Genesis 30:1-23 *Jacob's children*
- ☐ Day 19: Genesis 31:3-55 *Jacob's family leaves Laban*
- ☐ Day 20: Genesis 32—33 *Jacob and Esau reunite*
- ☐ Day 21: Genesis 35 *Jacob comes home; Isaac dies*
- ☐ Day 22: Genesis 37 *Joseph and his brothers*
- ☐ Day 23: Genesis 39 *Joseph in charge and in prison*
- ☐ Day 24: Genesis 40 *Joseph forgotten*
- ☐ Day 25: Genesis 41 *Joseph in charge*
- ☐ Day 26: Genesis 42 *Joseph's brothers visit*
- ☐ Day 27: Genesis 43 *Joseph's brothers visit again*
- ☐ Day 28: Genesis 44 *Joseph's brothers in trouble*
- ☐ Day 29: Genesis 45—46:7 *Joseph's forgiven family*
- ☐ Day 30: Genesis 49:29—50:26 *Jacob dies; Joseph dies*

19 Days with David

- ☐ Day 1: Ruth 1—2 *David's sad and hungry ancestors*
- ☐ Day 2: Ruth 3—4 *David's happy ancestors*
- ☐ Day 3: 1 Samuel 16 *David's anointing and new job*
- ☐ Day 4: Psalm 23 *David sings*
- ☐ Day 5: 1 Samuel 17 *David becomes a hero*
- ☐ Day 6: 1 Samuel 18:1-16 *David's best friend and worst enemy*

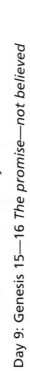

- Day 9: Matthew 5—6 Jesus talks to crowds about His kingdom
- Day 10: Matthew 7—8:13 Jesus teaches and heals two untouchables
- Day 11: Mark 4 Jesus tells stories and shows He is in charge of nature
- Day 12: Mark 5:21-43 Jesus heals and brings a dead girl back to life
- Day 13: Luke 9:10-17; John 6:1-15 Jesus feeds the hungry people
- Day 14: John 10:1-30; Luke 15:1-7 Jesus as the good shepherd
- Day 15: Matthew 13 Jesus' stories
- Day 16: Luke 15:8-32 Jesus tells about lost and found
- Day 17: Luke 18:15-17; Mark 10:13-16 Jesus and the children
- Day 18: Matthew 18:1-6,21-35 Greatness and forgiveness
- Day 19: Mark 10:17-31; Matthew 19:16-30 Jesus and a rich man
- Day 20: Mark 10:35-45 Jesus talks about His life and His death
- Day 21: Mark 14:1-11; John 12:1-11 Jesus prepares to die
- Day 22: John 12:12-19; Mark 11:1-11 Jesus enters Jerusalem as King
- Day 23: Mark 14:12-51 Jesus' last meal with His disciples; betrayal in the garden
- Day 24: Mark 14:53-72; 15:1-15 Jesus is tried and mocked
- Day 25: Mark 15:16-47 Jesus is crucified
- Day 26: John 20:1-18; Luke 24:1-12 Jesus is risen!
- Day 27: Luke 24:13-49; John 20:19-31 Jesus comes to His friends
- Day 28: John 21 Jesus restores Peter
- Day 29: Matthew 28:16-20; Luke 24:50-53 Jesus returns to heaven
- Day 30: Acts 1:1-11; 2:1-12,36-47 Jesus sends His Spirit; His family grows

- Day 7: 1 Samuel 18:17—19:18 David's wife; he runs for his life
- Day 8: 1 Samuel 20 Jonathan saves David's life
- Day 9: 1 Samuel 24 David spares Saul's life
- Day 10: 1 Samuel 31:1-7, 2 Samuel 5:1-10 David becomes king
- Day 11: 2 Samuel 22:1-20; Psalm 18:1-19 David rejoices
- Day 12: 2 Samuel 8:15—9:13 David reigns
- Day 13: 2 Samuel 11—12:25 David sins and is restored
- Day 14: 2 Samuel 15:1-30 Absalom tries to take the throne
- Day 15: 2 Samuel 18:1-10; 19:11-30 Absalom dies and David returns
- Day 16: 1 Kings 1:28-40 David makes Solomon king
- Day 17: 2 Samuel 23:1-4; 1 Kings 2:1-4,10-12 David dies
- Day 18: Psalm 27, Psalm 145 Songs David wrote
- Day 19: Matthew 1—2:12 David's family line to Jesus

30 Days with Jesus

- Day 1: John 1:1-14 Before Jesus came to Earth
- Day 2: Luke 1:26-56; Matthew 1:18-24 Mary and Joseph get the news
- Day 3: Luke 2:1-38; Matthew 2 Kings bring gifts; the family escapes to Egypt
- Day 4: Luke 2:41-52 Jesus grows into a young man
- Day 5: Luke 3:1-18; Matthew 3:13—4:17 Jesus begins to preach
- Day 6: John 1:29-50; Matthew 4:18-22 Jesus gathers disciples
- Day 7: John 2:1-11; Mark 1:21-45 Jesus does miracles
- Day 8: John 3:1-30; 4:1-42 Jesus talks one-on-one

STUDY SMART!

There are a zillion ways to study the Bible. But two kinds of books will help you learn what the Bible has to say about a particular topic: Bible dictionaries and concordances.

• **Want to know what "redemption" means? What a locust looks like?** Grab a **Bible dictionary!** It's a dictionary that explains the main words found in the Bible (in alphabetical order—it's easy!). It may also contain drawings, pictures, diagrams and places listed in the Bible (with maps!).

• **Where in the Bible can you find the word "sheep"? Where does the Bible tell about the oil and flour jars that didn't get empty?** A *concordance* is the place! It lists words found in the Bible in alphabetical order. Beside each word, Bible references tell where the word is found. A concordance may include only key words (words most people remember from the verse); many Bibles contain a key word concordance. But an *exhaustive* concordance includes *every* word—and weighs several pounds! (Online concordances are weightless!)

IMPORTANT NOTE: Find out which version of the Bible you have. Most concordances are written for a *specific version.* If you are using a *New Living Translation* (*NLT*), you need a concordance for the *NLT.* If you are using a concordance for the *King James Version* (*KJV*), but have an *NLT* Bible, you might or might not find the exact word you want.

Jesus promised us that the Holy Spirit will guide us into understanding what is true. So be sure to ask Him to help you every time you study God's Word!

For about 450 years, there was pretty much one version of the Bible in English. It was translated in 1611 under the direction of King James I of England. The translation was so good that everyone understood it quite well—until the twentieth century. Because language changes over time, many people in the twentieth century didn't understand the *King James Version* very well. So translations of the Bible into more modern English were begun. The *New International Version (NIV)*, the *New American Standard Version (NASB)*, and the *Contemporary English Version (CEV)* are just three of these modern Bibles. There are many others. There are also *paraphrases* available, such as *THE MESSAGE*; paraphrases tell the thoughts of the Bible but are not translations of the original words from Hebrew and Greek.

What's up with all these versions of the SAME book?

• **What does Jesus' story of the lost sheep mean?** Here's where **commentaries** are your friends! Reading a section of a commentary is kind of like reading a short sermon about a Bible passage. It explains details you might not have noticed or things you don't understand. On a commentary page, a Bible reference is listed (usually in bold print and usually at the top). The commentary then explains meanings and insights about that reference, phrase by phrase.

Commentaries are not just for pastors—they're for everyone! There are thousands of commentaries, from simple to complicated ones. Try online commentaries for free! (But be sure your online commentary comes from a person your parents or pastor are familiar with before you trust what he or she says!)

• **Would it help me to write my *own* book?** Yes! **Journaling** (writing about what we read in God's Word) helps us to remember and understand the Bible better. In fact, personal Bible study is where many commentaries got started! Use the Amazing Itty-Bitty Spiritual Exercise Journal (p. 73) or one of the How to Study the Bible pages (pp. 65-67) for simple ways to start *journaling* about what God teaches you. Add your prayer requests, too; then, look back at the requests from time to time to write down ways God answered—that's the true story of how God is at work in your own life!

cut   cut

CHAMPIONS
Colossians 2:6-7

WHERE I CAN GO...

When I'm worried about what I don't have:
Matthew 6:25,33

When I don't know what to say to God:
Romans 8:26

When I need to remember who is in control:
Romans 8:28

When it's hard to like another person:
Romans 15:7

When I'm tempted to worry:
Philippians 4:6-7

When I need to know what to do:
James 1:5

KEEP ON FOLLOWING JESUS!

CHAMPIONS
Colossians 2:6-7

WHERE I CAN GO...

When I'm worried about what I don't have:
Matthew 6:25,33

When I don't know what to say to God:
Romans 8:26

When I need to remember who is in control:
Romans 8:28

When it's hard to like another person:
Romans 15:7

When I'm tempted to worry:
Philippians 4:6-7

When I need to know what to do:
James 1:5

KEEP ON FOLLOWING JESUS!

CHAMPIONS
Colossians 2:6-7

WHERE I CAN GO...

When I'm worried about what I don't have:
Matthew 6:25,33

When I don't know what to say to God:
Romans 8:26

When I need to remember who is in control:
Romans 8:28

When it's hard to like another person:
Romans 15:7

When I'm tempted to worry:
Philippians 4:6-7

When I need to know what to do:
James 1:5

KEEP ON FOLLOWING JESUS!

CHAMPIONS
Colossians 2:6-7

WHERE I CAN GO...

When I'm worried about what I don't have:
Matthew 6:25,33

When I don't know what to say to God:
Romans 8:26

When I need to remember who is in control:
Romans 8:28

When it's hard to like another person:
Romans 15:7

When I'm tempted to worry:
Philippians 4:6-7

When I need to know what to do:
James 1:5

KEEP ON FOLLOWING JESUS!

CHAMPIONS
Colossians 2:6-7

WHERE I CAN GO...

When I'm worried about what I don't have:
Matthew 6:25,33

When I don't know what to say to God:
Romans 8:26

When I need to remember who is in control:
Romans 8:28

When it's hard to like another person:
Romans 15:7

When I'm tempted to worry:
Philippians 4:6-7

When I need to know what to do:
James 1:5

KEEP ON FOLLOWING JESUS!

CHAMPIONS
Colossians 2:6-7

WHERE I CAN GO...

When I'm worried about what I don't have:
Matthew 6:25,33

When I don't know what to say to God:
Romans 8:26

When I need to remember who is in control:
Romans 8:28

When it's hard to like another person:
Romans 15:7

When I'm tempted to worry:
Philippians 4:6-7

When I need to know what to do:
James 1:5

KEEP ON FOLLOWING JESUS!

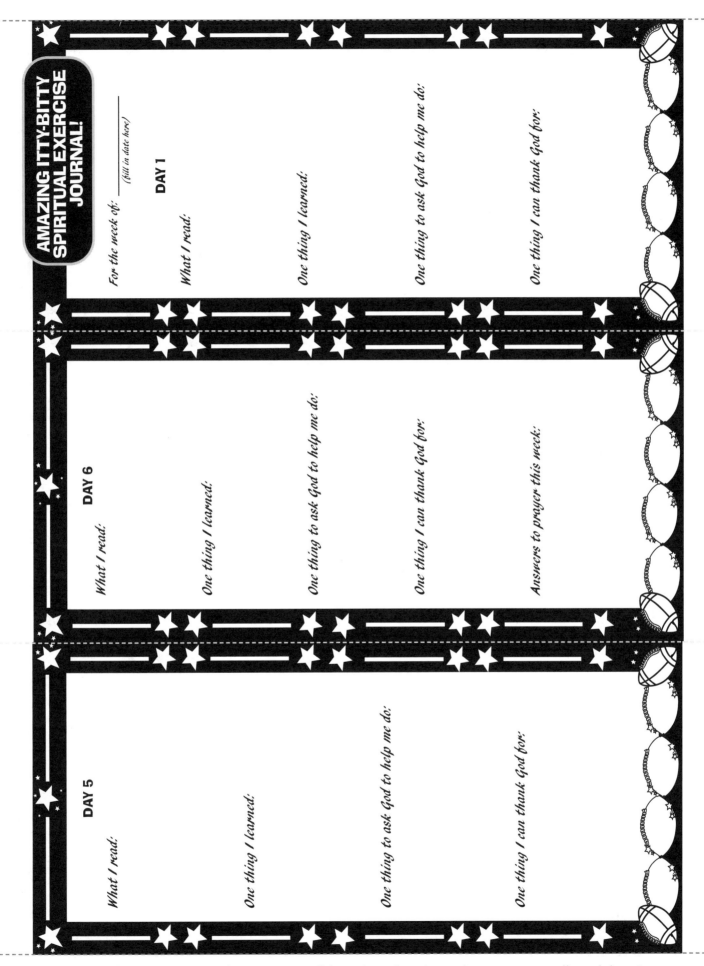

AMAZING ITTY-BITTY SPIRITUAL EXERCISE JOURNAL!

For the week of: _____
(fill in date here)

DAY 1

What I read:

One thing I learned:

One thing to ask God to help me do:

One thing I can thank God for:

DAY 6

What I read:

One thing I learned:

One thing to ask God to help me do:

One thing I can thank God for:

Answers to prayer this week:

DAY 5

What I read:

One thing I learned:

One thing to ask God to help me do:

One thing I can thank God for:

Accordion-fold this page, tuck it into your Bible and use it to journal your progress all week long!

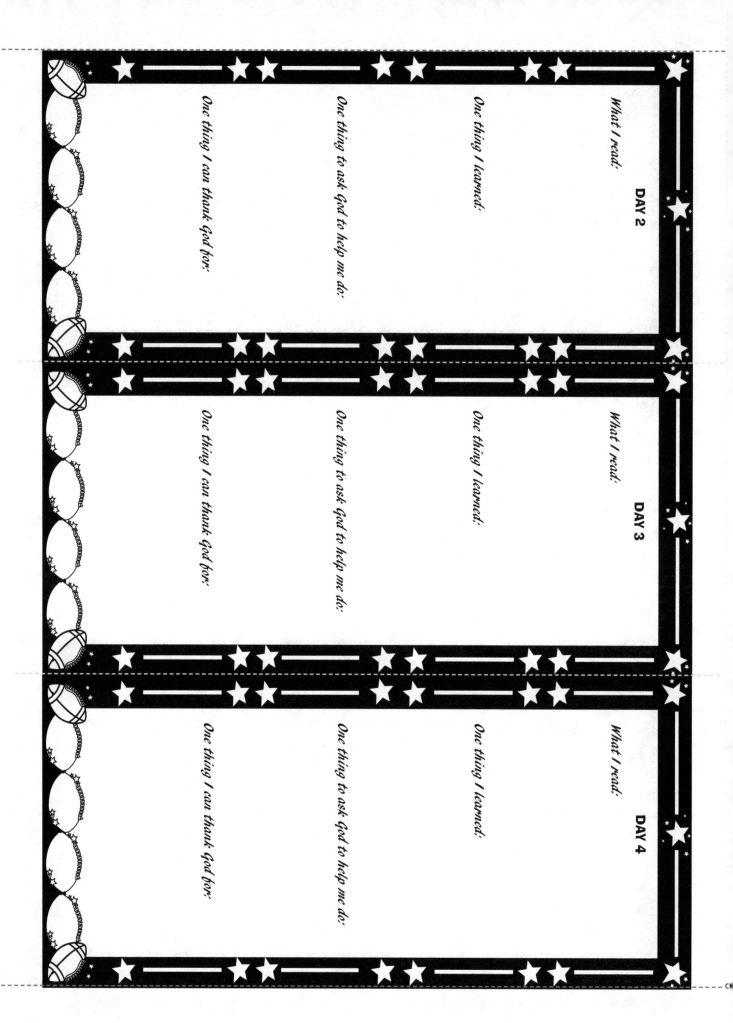

DAY 2

What I read:

One thing I learned:

One thing to ask God to help me do:

One thing I can thank God for:

DAY 3

What I read:

One thing I learned:

One thing to ask God to help me do:

One thing I can thank God for:

DAY 4

What I read:

One thing I learned:

One thing to ask God to help me do:

One thing I can thank God for:

EXODUS 20:3-17

"You shall have no other gods before me" (Exodus 20:3).

"You shall not make for yourself an idol . . . You shall not bow down to them or worship them" (Exodus 20:4-5).

"You shall not misuse the name of the LORD your God" (Exodus 20:7).

"Remember the Sabbath day by keeping it holy" (Exodus 20:8).

"Honor your father and your mother, so that you may live long" (Exodus 20:12).

"You shall not murder" (Exodus 20:13).

"You shall not commit adultery" (Exodus 20:14).

"You shall not steal" (Exodus 20:15).

"You shall not give false testimony against your neighbor" (Exodus 20:16).

"You shall not covet" (Exodus 20:17).

Psalm 23

"The LORD is my shepherd, I shall not be in want. He makes me lie down in green pastures, he leads me beside quiet waters, he restores my soul. He guides me in paths of righteousness for his name's sake. Even though I walk through the valley of the shadow of death, I will fear no evil, for you are with me; your rod and your staff, they comfort me. You prepare a table before me in the presence of my enemies. You anoint my head with oil; my cup overflows. Surely goodness and love will follow me all the days of my life, and I will dwell in the house of the LORD forever."

Psalm 100

"Shout for joy to the LORD, all the earth. Worship the LORD with gladness; come before him with joyful songs. Know that the LORD is God. It is he who made us, and we are his; we are his people, the sheep of his pasture. Enter his gates with thanksgiving and his courts with praise; give thanks to him and praise his name. For the LORD is good and his love endures forever; his faithfulness continues through all generations."

Matthew 5:3-9

"Blessed are the poor in spirit, for theirs is the kingdom of heaven. Blessed are those who mourn, for they will be comforted. Blessed are the meek, for they will inherit the earth. Blessed are those who hunger and thirst for righteousness, for they will be filled. Blessed are the merciful, for they will be shown mercy. Blessed are the pure in heart, for they will see God. Blessed are the peacemakers, for they will be called sons of God."

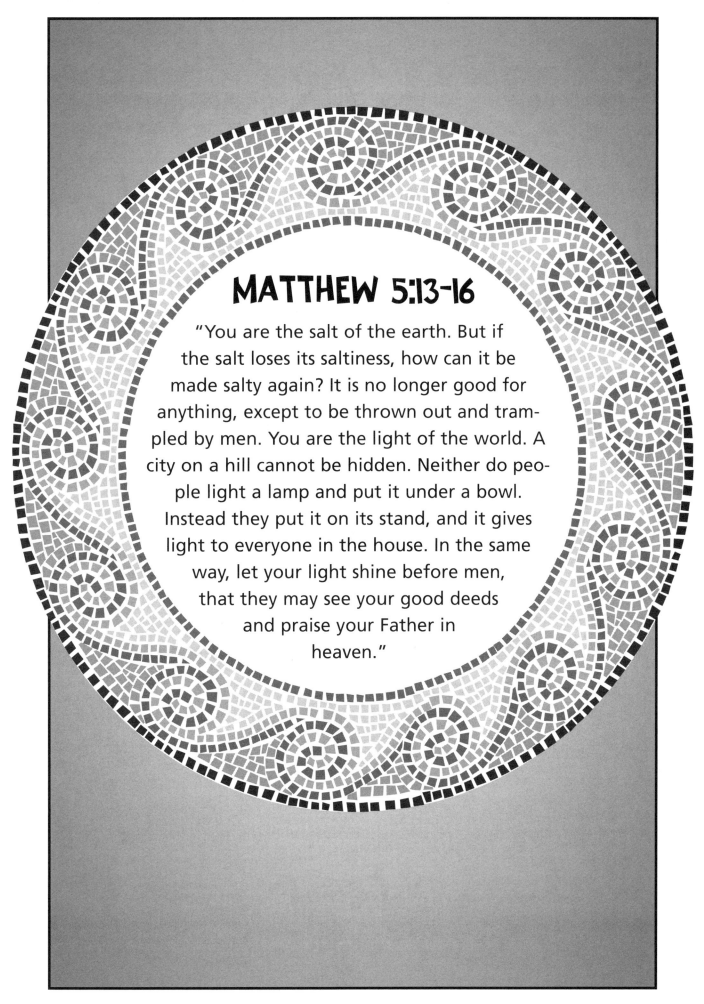

MATTHEW 5:13-16

"You are the salt of the earth. But if the salt loses its saltiness, how can it be made salty again? It is no longer good for anything, except to be thrown out and trampled by men. You are the light of the world. A city on a hill cannot be hidden. Neither do people light a lamp and put it under a bowl. Instead they put it on its stand, and it gives light to everyone in the house. In the same way, let your light shine before men, that they may see your good deeds and praise your Father in heaven."

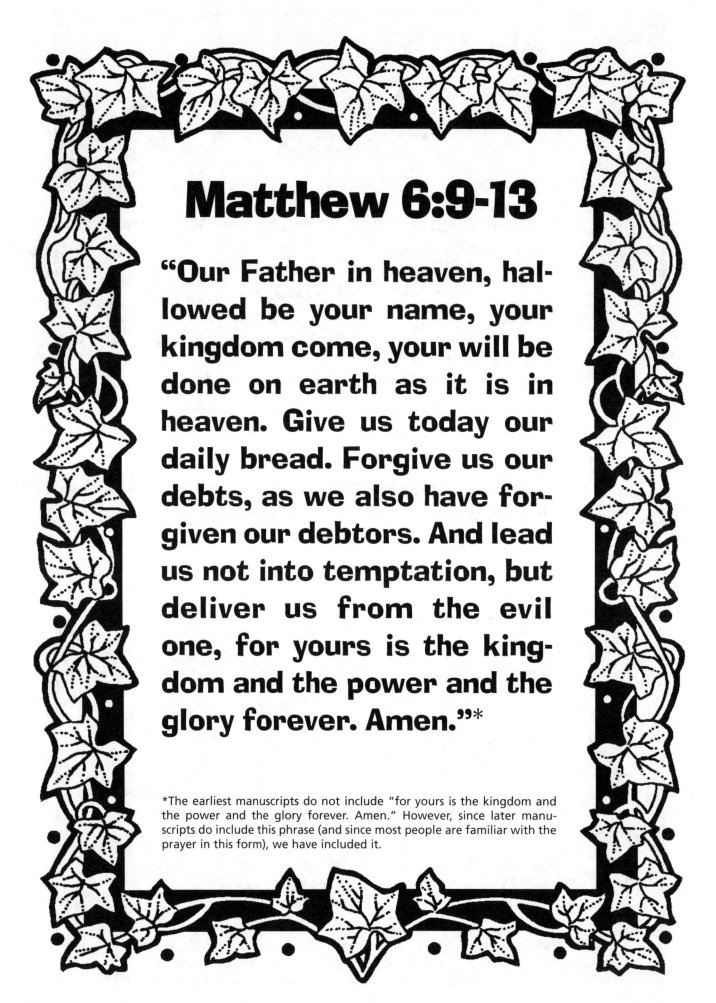

Matthew 6:9-13

"Our Father in heaven, hallowed be your name, your kingdom come, your will be done on earth as it is in heaven. Give us today our daily bread. Forgive us our debts, as we also have forgiven our debtors. And lead us not into temptation, but deliver us from the evil one, for yours is the kingdom and the power and the glory forever. Amen."*

*The earliest manuscripts do not include "for yours is the kingdom and the power and the glory forever. Amen." However, since later manuscripts do include this phrase (and since most people are familiar with the prayer in this form), we have included it.

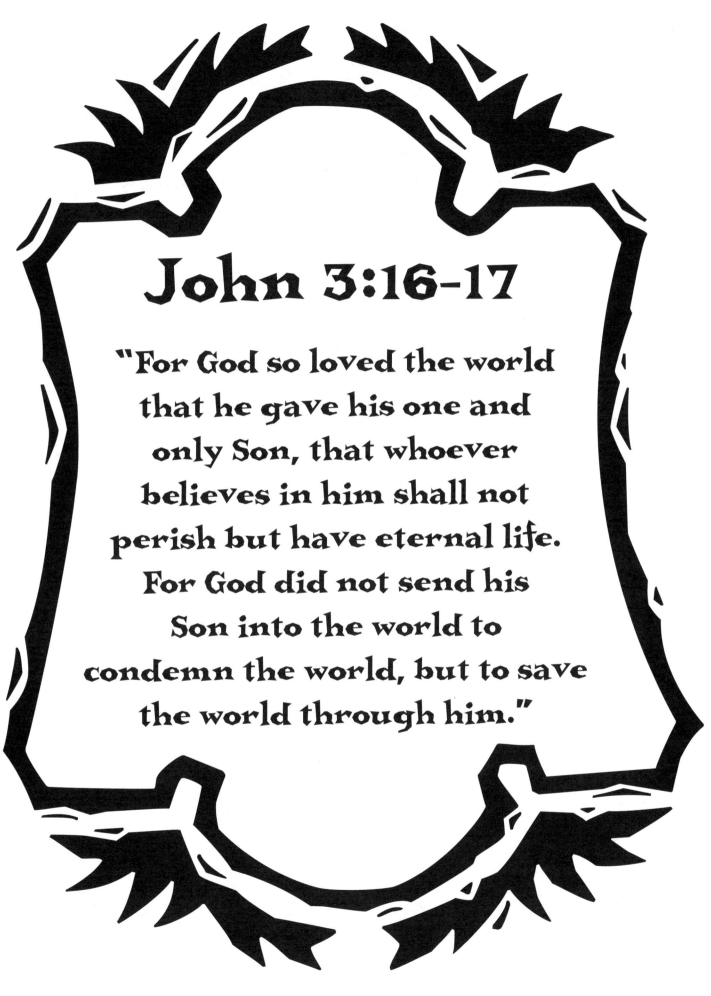

John 3:16-17

"For God so loved the world that he gave his one and only Son, that whoever believes in him shall not perish but have eternal life. For God did not send his Son into the world to condemn the world, but to save the world through him."

1 Corinthians 13:4-8

"Love is patient, love is kind. It does not envy, it does not boast, it is not proud. It is not rude, it is not self-seeking, it is not easily angered, it keeps no record of wrongs. Love does not delight in evil but rejoices with the truth. It always protects, always trusts, always hopes, always perseveres. Love never fails."

Galatians 5:22-23

"The fruit of the Spirit is love, joy, peace, patience, kindness, goodness, faithfulness, gentleness and self-control. Against such things there is no law."

1 John 1:9-10

"If we confess our sins, he is faithful and just and will forgive us our sins and purify us from all unrighteousness. If we claim we have not sinned, we make him out to be a liar and his word has no place in our lives."

The World of Earth's Most Amazing Book

Simply fascinating. Shall we go?

EVERYDAY LIFE IN BIBLE TIMES

"Snapshots" of information selected to increase understanding of aspects of the daily lives and times of Bible people.

Plants

The climate in Israel and the surrounding countries is cooler and wetter near the coast, hotter and drier inland. Here are some of the plants grown and ways people use them!

Grains such as millet, barley, wheat, buckwheat are all for eating!

Reeds grow near water; their fiber is used to make a kind of paper.

Flax plants grow lovely blue flowers and fiber used to make linen cloth.

Olive trees grow olives for eating, olive oil and wood.

Date Roll Ups

Remove the pits and flatten dates into a very thin circle. Let dry in the sun for 2 days and roll up.

Fig trees grow leathery brownish or black figs, sweet and full of tiny seeds. Good for eating and even for medicine. (Can you find the story about a time when a fig poultice [POLE tus], or medicine, was used?*)

Palm trees produce fiber (for weaving into mats, baskets and ropes) and dates for eating.

*See 2 Kings 20:7 for the story!

Animals

The Bible was written a long time ago—before motors, cars, airplanes or trains had been invented. Animals did most of the work machines do now. Animals also provided food (eggs, milk and meat) and fiber (wool and hair for clothing, tents, rugs, etc.). Here are some animals that were part of the lives of people who lived in Bible times.

Donkeys make good transportation and burden-carriers. (When did one carry Jesus?**)

Camels are good long-distance transportation animals that also provide milk and hair. (Who wore clothes made of camel's hair?*)

Goats are herded along with sheep and provide milk, hair and meat.

Quail are small native birds. God sent flocks of them to feed the Israelites in the desert!***

Scorpions are small and poisonous—one might not kill you but it can hurt you!

Ravens are wild birds that usually eat dead things. But God sent ravens to Elijah—carrying fresh food!

Sheep are raised for milk, wool and meat.

*See Matthew 3:1-6 for the answer! **See Mark 11:1-11 to get the story! ***Read Exodus 16 to find out more!

Travel

To travel from one place to another, most ordinary people used their feet!

It's the cheapest way to go!

There's no use hurrying—we can only walk so fast!

Litters carried wealthy people, using someone else's feet—the *easiest* way to go.

Camels traveled a long way over land; carried a lot of cargo; can go for days without water.

Ships traveled a long distance *across* water. Pay for a place but bring your own food—this is *not* a cruise!

Chariots carried messengers, soldiers or people in a big hurry. When pulled by swift horses, it was the *fastest* way to go!

Clothing and Shoes

How many shirts do you own? How many pairs of shoes?

In Bible times, making cloth took a great deal of work. So clothing was worn, passed on and worn some more until it wore out (then people used the scraps!).

Basic pieces of clothing:

Tunic short-sleeved for workers. Long-sleeved tunics were for bosses or for special-occasion clothes.

Cloak thrown around the shoulders. Some had sleeves; some did not.

Belt a long piece of fabric—wound, tucked and tied. Folds made useful pockets!

Shoes were sandals of many kinds. Richer people's sandals were made to fit their feet. Poorer people often got used sandals and sometimes carried them to make them last longer!

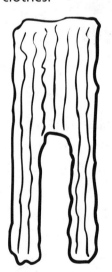 

Headgear kept hair clean and sweat out of the eyes. No one left home without it! Different styles indicated what a man's job was. Women's headgear showed whether a lady was single, married or widowed!

Mantle laid over the shoulders, tied at the waist

Roman clothing was different. It often showed the country from which a person had come.

Food

Imagine a world with no fast-food restaurants!

Common foods in Bible times:

Fruit, like melons, apples, figs, grapes, dates and pomegranates, grew well!

Roasted grain makes a great travel snack!

Grain wheat, barley, millet, buckwheat were boiled, roasted or ground into flour for bread.

Nuts, like almonds and pistachios, for eating raw or roasted.

Vegetables, like squashes, spinach, eggplant, onions, garlic, are still delicious!

Beans, especially lentils and chickpeas, made soups, dips and sauces.

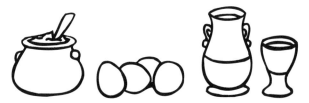

Other protein, eggs (of many birds, not just chickens), milk (even sheep's and camel's milk!) as well as cheese, butter, cream and yogurt, were eaten.

Sweets were mainly honey, raisins and dates! Or dabs (syrup made from raisins).

Animal protein (fish, chicken, lamb and beef) was eaten, but the richer you were, the more animal protein you could afford to eat.

But NO pork, camel or rabbit! No crab or lobster!*

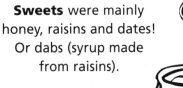

*Look at Leviticus 11 for more about what God's people did and did not eat.

What About Water?

We turn on a faucet and clean, drinkable water comes out.

Israel is a fairly dry, hot country. Where did Bible-times people get clean water?

Wells are holes dug deep enough to reach an aquifer (the underground layer where water is stored). Wells were the main source of water for most towns.

Wells were also an important part of town life. Women usually went to draw the day's water from the well together, early in the day—it was a good time to talk!

Cisterns are holes in the ground for storing rainwater. (Who sat in a cistern?*)

Springs are what people sometimes called "living water" because the water flows out of the ground by itself.

Aqueducts are channels built to carry water from springs into cities.

Drought (say, "drowt") is what happens when it doesn't rain for a long time. Plants die. Then animals die. Then the aquifers go dry. It's not a pretty picture.

*See Genesis 37:23-24. **See 2 Kings 20:20.

Homes

Where does your family live? In Bible times (and for **nomads**, or wandering people) home might be wherever your tent was!

Tents were made of skins or of cloth made from goat hair. Portable!

Need more space? Make the tent larger!

Flat roofs were what most houses had, good for drying crops or clothes and also for catching cool evening breezes!

Houses were mostly made of mud bricks or of **daub and wattle** (sticks woven together and then plastered with mud).

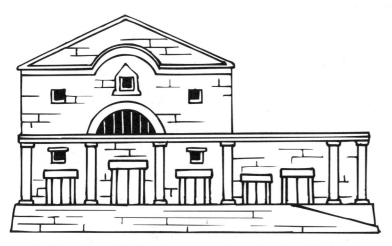

Palaces and Temples were often made of stone blocks. (That's why many can still be seen today!)

The Temple at Jerusalem was made of cut stone blocks. They were cut to fit together exactly. They were then transported to the Temple site and fit together at the site like a big puzzle!

Right at Home!

Once upon a time, there were no TVs or computers, no washing machines or telephones . . .

Clay pots were for water and storing grain, flour, oil, etc.

Bowls and **cups** haven't changed much!

Lamps were usually made of clay. Oil, which was poured into the bottom, was pulled up into the wick; the wick was then lit.

Tables, benches, chairs are still used!

Ovens (where food was cooked) might be indoors and outside the house, too.

Rugs and **blankets** were for sitting on and sleeping in.

Work, Part 1

People have worked ever since they were created! (What jobs did God give Adam to do in the Garden of Eden?*)

In Bible times, jobs included . . .

Stonecutters, who cut stone from a quarry and built stone buildings.

Carpenters, who made furniture and did home repairs.

Scribes, who did reading and writing for nonreaders.

Weavers, who made cloth, blankets, rugs, tent fabric.

Brick makers, who also built brick walls and buildings.

Tentmakers, who also repaired tents. (This was Paul's side job. Who else made tents?**)

Priests, who could only do this job if they were Aaron's descendants!***

* See Genesis 2:15,19. ** See Acts 18:1-3. ***See Exodus 29:44.

Work, Part 2: Farmer, Shepherd, Fisherman

Jesus often told stories about these familiar jobs!

Plow soil to soften and make furrows for seeds.

Sow (toss) seeds into furrows; cover seeds with soil.

Wait and pray for rain and not too much heat!

Cut ripe grain with a scythe (say, "SIGHth").

Farming from seed to bread!

Tie into sheaves (bundles).

Thresh (crush) to remove outer coat or "chaff" from grain. Animals help!

Winnow (toss) grain so wind blows chaff away, while grain falls.

Grind into flour—yes, that *is* a heavy stone wheel!

Bake (mix flour with yeast, warm water and a little sugar. Knead, wait for dough to rise, then shape and bake).

Eat!

Shepherding

Many families kept a flock of sheep. The youngest members of the family were usually the shepherds. (Which youngest son and shepherd became a king?*)

Others raised sheep to sell. A shepherd had to lead sheep to good grass and clean water, drive off predators (animals that eat sheep), find lost sheep, care for sick or wounded sheep—it was a 24/7 job!

Sheepfolds were built by shepherds to protect sheep during the night. (Read John 10 for more about shepherds and sheepfolds!)

THWAK! YELP! HOWL! YOWL!

Fishing

Families living near a lake or an ocean might fish, make ropes or nets, build boats or prepare and sell dried fish.

Fishing could be done by casting a net while standing near the shore or by dropping nets from a boat.

* See 1 Samuel 16:11-13.

Government
Government in Old Testament Times

A Family

God promised Abraham that He would make a great nation from Abraham's descendants. Abraham's family grew in number to 70 by the time Joseph ruled in Egypt (see Genesis 46:26-27).

A Nation

The family grew into a nation in Egypt, where they lived for over 400 years. When God led them back toward Canaan (the Promised Land), He promised to be their ONLY king. During this time, Moses appointed men to be judges to help people settle their disagreements (see Exodus 18:13-26).

Judges

When the people came to Canaan (where Abraham had first lived), Joshua led them under God's kingship. But after Joshua died, Israel forgot to obey God and worshiped idols. Then, when trouble came, they remembered God and asked for His help. God helped Israel through leaders He sent. Their stories are in the book of Judges. Israel would disobey again and again; then, each time trouble came, they would remember God and He would send a person to help and lead them.

Kings

Samuel was the last judge. When he got old, the people asked for a human king. (Read the story in 1 Samuel 8.) God sent Samuel to anoint Saul as the first king. Later, David became king. Then his son Solomon ruled as king.

Division and Captivity

After Solomon, the kingdom split into two: The 10 tribes living in the north were called Israel. The 2 tribes living in the south were called Judah. Both kingdoms had a series of kings; some obeyed God but many did not. In 722 B.C. Assyria attacked Israel. Many of the people were taken to Assyria and never returned to their homeland. Later, many of the people of Judah were taken captive to Babylon. But after 70 years in Babylon, some of these people returned.

Return and Domination

By the end of Old Testament times, the people who had returned to Judah had rebuilt the cities and the Temple. During the time between the Old and New Testaments, the Greeks, the Egyptians (Ptolemies) and the Seleucids controlled the country as a small part of bigger empires. By the time Jesus lived there, the country was part of the Roman Empire.

Government Workers in Jesus' Day

Tax collectors worked for the Roman Empire. They were NOT very well liked because they were part of the mean Roman government. Besides, they took more tax money than Rome demanded— and kept the extra!

That tax collector took all my chickens— and my donkey, too!

Roman soldiers lived in many places around the country.

Centurions were Roman commanders of a **century** (80 to 100 soldiers).

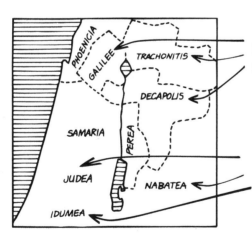

Herod was the Roman governor over northern Israel.

Pontius Pilate was the Roman governor over southern Israel.

The Sanhedrin was the ruling group of 70 Jewish leaders. They could make some rules, but Rome had the final say about laws.

+ 68

Worship

In old Testament times (before Jesus), God's people worshiped Him in some ways that were different from ways we worship today.

Sacrifices (gifts) brought by people to be offered to God by the priests.

Priests also burned **incense** as a sacrifice to thank God.

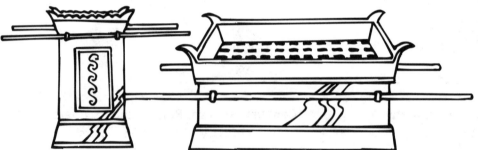

Incense altar   Sacrifice altar

Sin offerings (animals) brought to be offered to God by the priests to pay for people's sins.

The Bible says that when Jesus took the punishment for our sins, it was a once-for-all sacrifice. No other sacrifice *ever* had to be offered for sin again!

Some ways God's people worship Him have never changed!

We still

Pray and **sing** to praise God and ask Him for what we need!

Read God's Word to learn more about Him.

Jesus is our hope.

Listen to teachings to understand His Word better.

Fellowship by being together, showing love and having fun!

Celebrate communion or **baptism** to show our love and obedience.

Give to show our love for God and others.

idol Worship

In the Ten Commandments, God told His people first that they were to worship Him alone. Then God told His people not to make any idols or to worship them.

But Israel didn't always obey.

Sometimes they worshiped gods of the people who lived near them.

Sometimes they worshiped idols that looked like birds or animals.

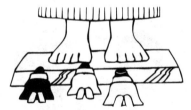

Sometimes they worshiped BIG idols. But God said NO IDOLS!

What do many people today worship (trust in, pray to, think about) instead of God? Anything (like money, toys, being popular, having a cool house) can be an idol. God wants us to show we love Him more than anything else!

Holidays

What holidays does your family celebrate? In Bible times, God's people were COMMANDED to celebrate holidays! (The Bible calls these holidays "feasts.")

God told them to come together to thank Him, to spend time together and to rest from their work.*

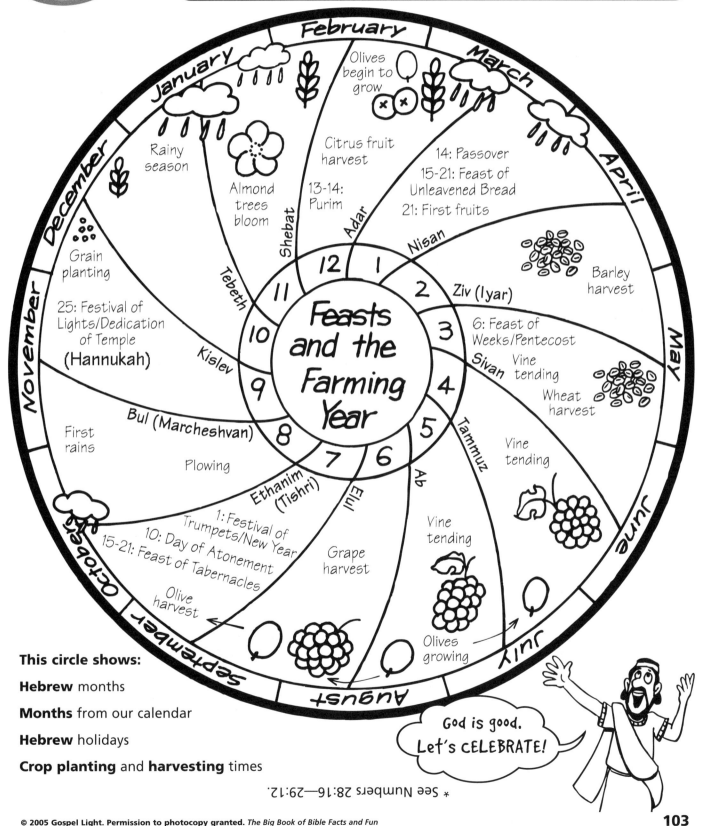

Feasts and the Farming Year

January — Rainy season — Almond trees bloom
February — Olives begin to grow — Citrus fruit harvest — 13-14: Purim
March — 14: Passover — 15-21: Feast of Unleavened Bread — 21: First fruits
April — Barley harvest
May — 6: Feast of Weeks/Pentecost — Vine tending — Wheat harvest
June — Vine tending
July — Olives growing
August — Vine tending — Grape harvest
September — Olive harvest
October — 1: Festival of Trumpets/New Year — 10: Day of Atonement — 15-21: Feast of Tabernacles
November — First rains — Plowing
December — Grain planting — 25: Festival of Lights/Dedication of Temple (Hannukah)

Hebrew months: 1 Nisan, 2 Ziv (Iyar), 3 Sivan, 4 Tammuz, 5 Ab, 6 Elul, 7 Ethanim (Tishri), 8 Bul (Marcheshvan), 9 Kislev, 10 Tebeth, 11 Shebat, 12 Adar

This circle shows:

Hebrew months

Months from our calendar

Hebrew holidays

Crop planting and **harvesting** times

God is good. Let's CELEBRATE!

* See Numbers 28:16—29:12.

Musical Instruments

Here are some of the musical instruments that were common in Bible times. Which ones are the most like instruments we play today?

Lyre the guitar may have come from this

Harp open on one side

Tambourine to shake and hit!

Trumpet two kinds: ram's horn and metal

Cymbals ranging from tiny to large in size

What musical instrument do you always have with you?*

Flute a little different from today's flutes

* Your voice!

Bible Maps

Where in the world did the events of Earth's Most Amazing Book history take place?

?

?

Japan?

?

?

NEW YORK?

SOUTH AMERICA?

A series of "big pictures" to help students understand the areas where Bible history took place and the movements of God's people from one place to another! Also includes in-depth map puzzle challenges for students!

MAP

Map of the Beginnings

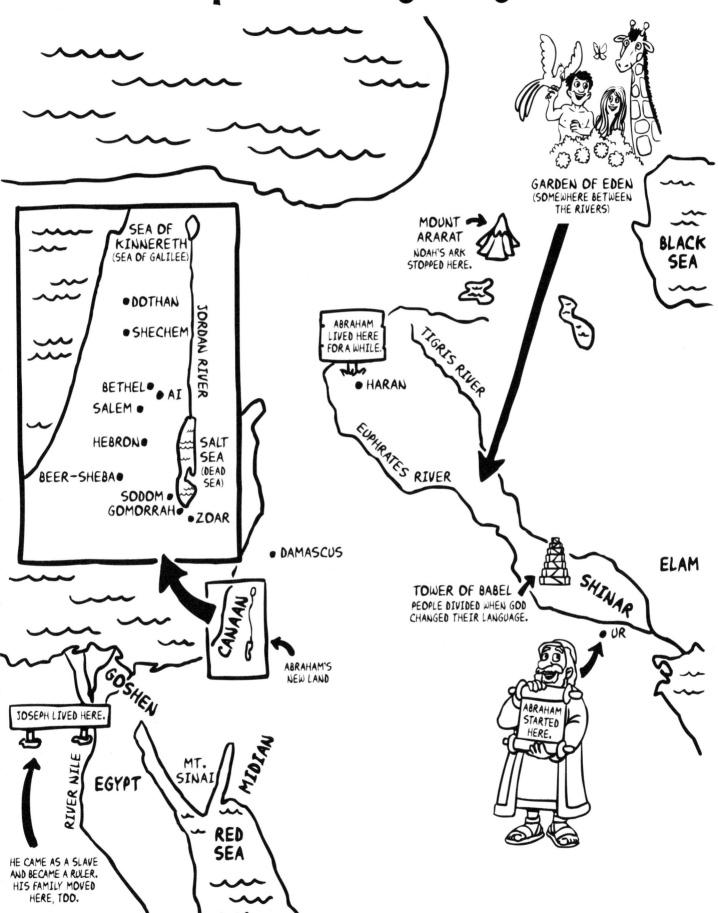

GARDEN OF EDEN (SOMEWHERE BETWEEN THE RIVERS)

BLACK SEA

MOUNT ARARAT NOAH'S ARK STOPPED HERE.

SEA OF KINNERETH (SEA OF GALILEE)

DOTHAN

SHECHEM

JORDAN RIVER

BETHEL • AI
SALEM •

HEBRON •

SALT SEA (DEAD SEA)

BEER-SHEBA •

SODOM •
GOMORRAH • ZOAR

ABRAHAM LIVED HERE FOR A WHILE.

• HARAN

TIGRIS RIVER

EUPHRATES RIVER

• DAMASCUS

CANAAN

ABRAHAM'S NEW LAND

TOWER OF BABEL PEOPLE DIVIDED WHEN GOD CHANGED THEIR LANGUAGE.

SHINAR

ELAM

• UR

ABRAHAM STARTED HERE.

GOSHEN

JOSEPH LIVED HERE.

RIVER NILE

EGYPT

MT. SINAI

MIDIAN

RED SEA

HE CAME AS A SLAVE AND BECAME A RULER. HIS FAMILY MOVED HERE, TOO.

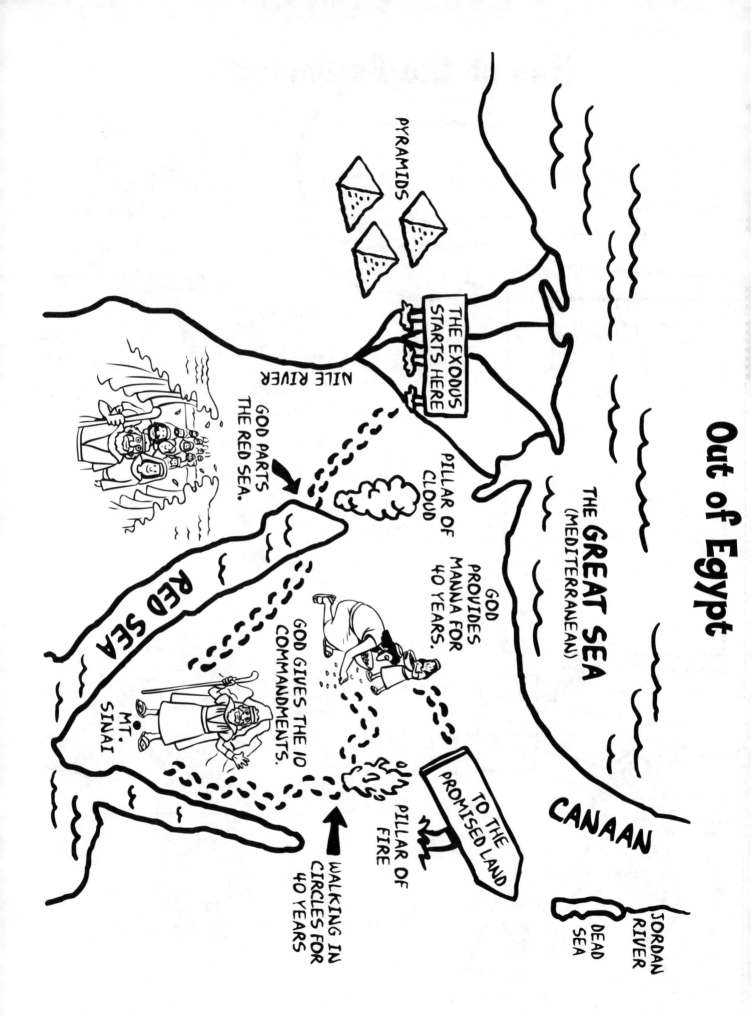

Out of Egypt

PYRAMIDS

THE EXODUS STARTS HERE

NILE RIVER

GOD PARTS THE RED SEA.

PILLAR OF CLOUD

THE **GREAT SEA** (MEDITERRANEAN)

GOD PROVIDES MANNA FOR 40 YEARS.

RED SEA

MT. SINAI

GOD GIVES THE 10 COMMANDMENTS.

CANAAN

TO THE PROMISED LAND

PILLAR OF FIRE

WALKING IN CIRCLES FOR 40 YEARS

JORDAN RIVER

DEAD SEA

The Conquest of Canaan

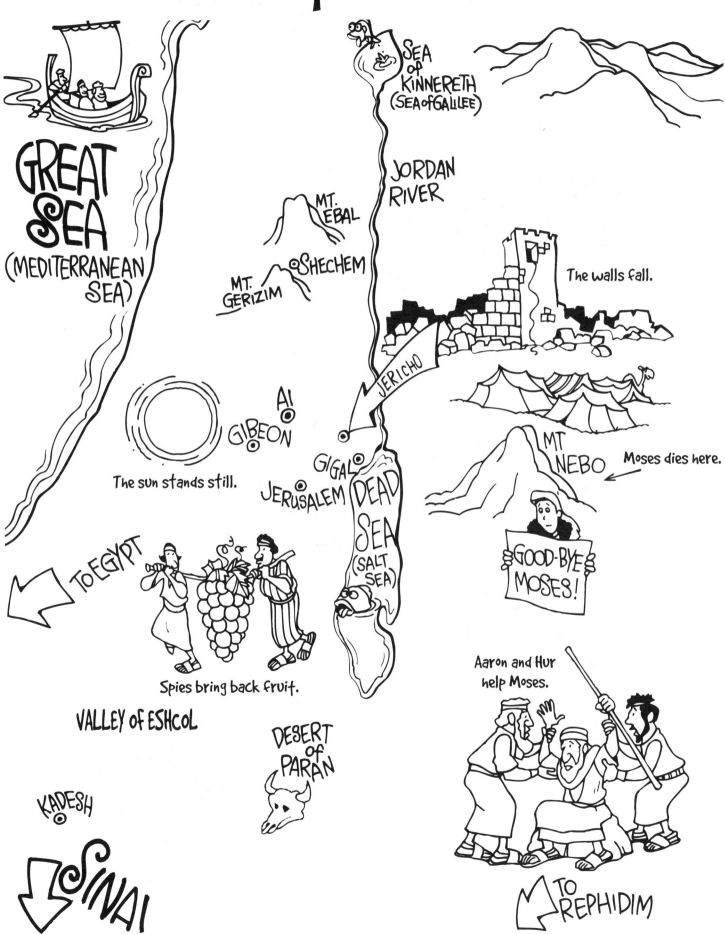

GREAT SEA (MEDITERRANEAN SEA)

SEA of KINNERETH (SEA of GALILEE)

JORDAN RIVER

MT. EBAL

SHECHEM

MT. GERIZIM

The walls fall.

JERICHO

AI

GIBEON

The sun stands still.

GIGAL

JERUSALEM

DEAD SEA (SALT SEA)

MT NEBO

Moses dies here.

GOOD-BYE MOSES!

TO EGYPT

Spies bring back fruit.

VALLEY of ESHCOL

DESERT of PARAN

Aaron and Hur help Moses.

KADESH

SINAI

TO REPHIDIM

The Land of the Tribes

(before there were kings)

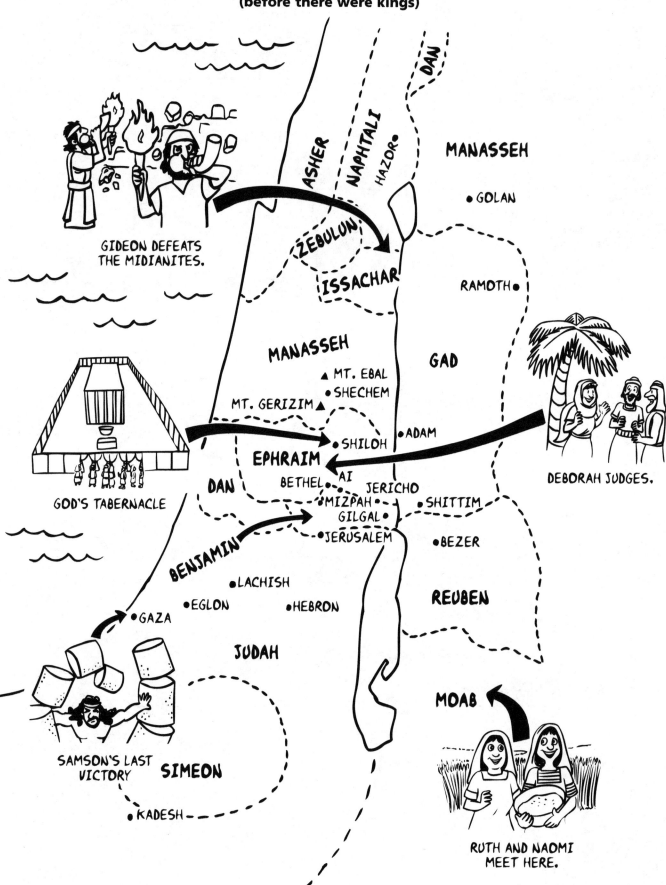

GIDEON DEFEATS THE MIDIANITES.

GOD'S TABERNACLE

SAMSON'S LAST VICTORY

DEBORAH JUDGES.

RUTH AND NAOMI MEET HERE.

ASHER

NAPHTALI

DAN

HAZOR

MANASSEH

GOLAN

ZEBULUN

ISSACHAR

RAMOTH

MANASSEH

MT. EBAL
SHECHEM
MT. GERIZIM

GAD

ADAM

SHILOH

EPHRAIM

DAN

BETHEL

AI

JERICHO

MIZPAH

SHITTIM

GILGAL

JERUSALEM

BEZER

BENJAMIN

LACHISH

REUBEN

EGLON

HEBRON

GAZA

JUDAH

MOAB

SIMEON

KADESH

israel Under Kings

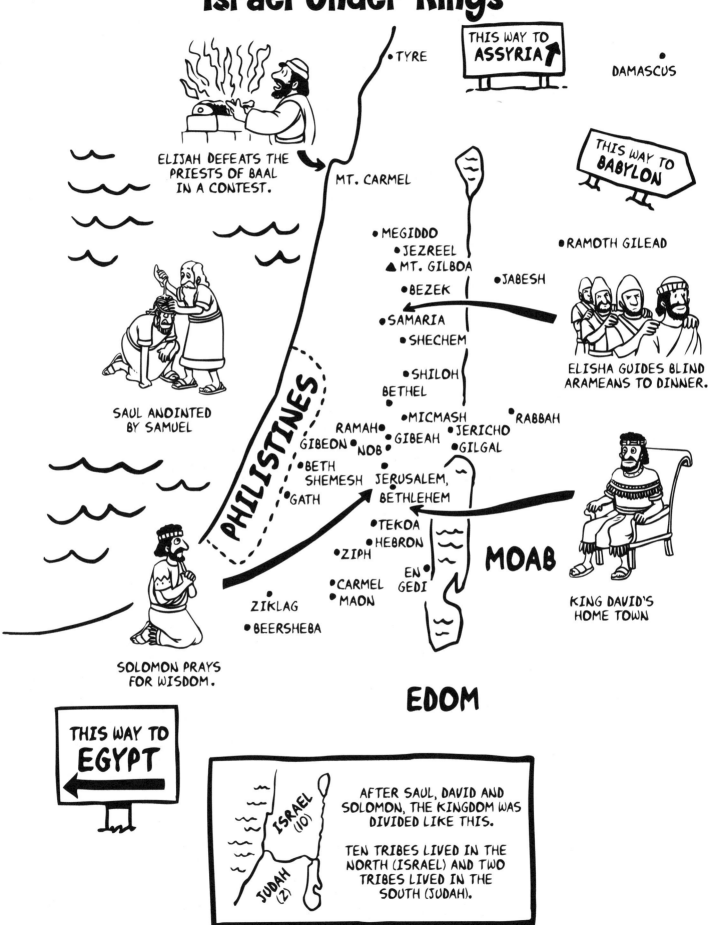

TYRE

THIS WAY TO ASSYRIA

DAMASCUS

ELIJAH DEFEATS THE PRIESTS OF BAAL IN A CONTEST.

MT. CARMEL

THIS WAY TO BABYLON

MEGIDDO
JEZREEL
MT. GILBOA
BEZEK
JABESH
SAMARIA
SHECHEM

RAMOTH GILEAD

SHILOH
BETHEL

SAUL ANOINTED BY SAMUEL

ELISHA GUIDES BLIND ARAMEANS TO DINNER.

PHILISTINES

MICMASH
RAMAH
GIBEON NOB GIBEAH
BETH SHEMESH
GATH
JERUSALEM, BETHLEHEM
JERICHO
GILGAL
RABBAH

TEKOA
HEBRON
ZIPH
EN GEDI
CARMEL MAON
ZIKLAG
BEERSHEBA

MOAB

KING DAVID'S HOME TOWN

SOLOMON PRAYS FOR WISDOM.

EDOM

THIS WAY TO EGYPT

ISRAEL (10)

JUDAH (2)

AFTER SAUL, DAVID AND SOLOMON, THE KINGDOM WAS DIVIDED LIKE THIS.

TEN TRIBES LIVED IN THE NORTH (ISRAEL) AND TWO TRIBES LIVED IN THE SOUTH (JUDAH).

To and From Babylon!

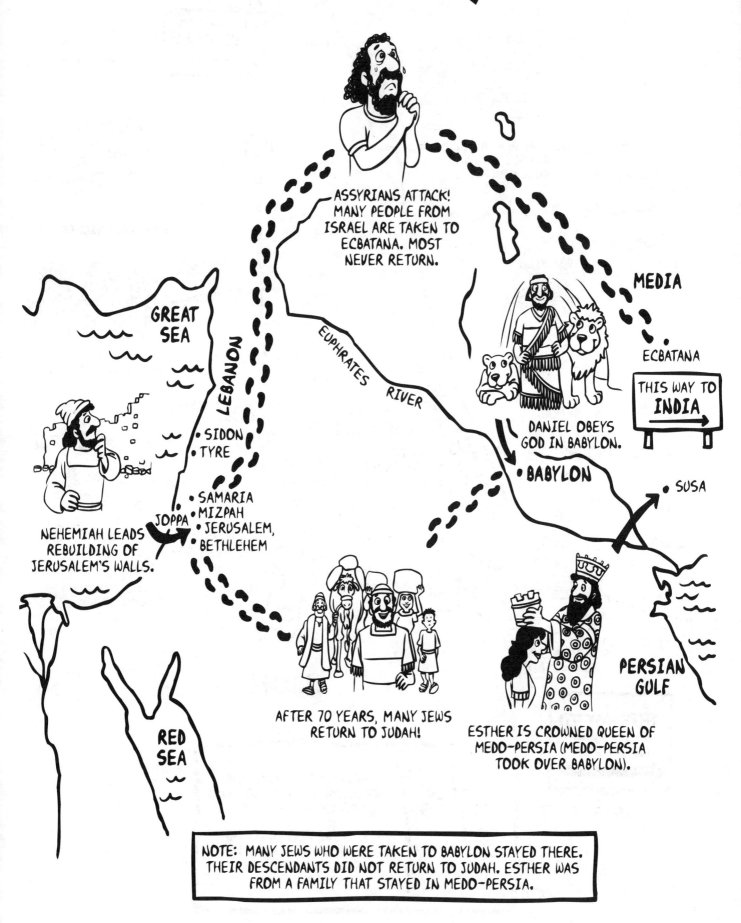

ASSYRIANS ATTACK! MANY PEOPLE FROM ISRAEL ARE TAKEN TO ECBATANA. MOST NEVER RETURN.

MEDIA

GREAT SEA

LEBANON

EUPHRATES RIVER

ECBATANA

THIS WAY TO INDIA

DANIEL OBEYS GOD IN BABYLON.

• SIDON
• TYRE

• BABYLON

• SUSA

• SAMARIA
• MIZPAH
JOPPA • JERUSALEM,
• BETHLEHEM

NEHEMIAH LEADS REBUILDING OF JERUSALEM'S WALLS.

AFTER 70 YEARS, MANY JEWS RETURN TO JUDAH!

ESTHER IS CROWNED QUEEN OF MEDO-PERSIA (MEDO-PERSIA TOOK OVER BABYLON).

PERSIAN GULF

RED SEA

NOTE: MANY JEWS WHO WERE TAKEN TO BABYLON STAYED THERE. THEIR DESCENDANTS DID NOT RETURN TO JUDAH. ESTHER WAS FROM A FAMILY THAT STAYED IN MEDO-PERSIA.

Jesus' Homeland

Jesus heals the official's son—long distance!
Jesus brings a dead girl back to life.

Mt. HERMON

GREAT SEA

CANA

CAPERNAUM

● CAESAREA PHILIPPI

● BETHSAIDA

SEA OF GALILEE

NAZARETH

Mt. TABOR

Jesus grew up here!

Samaria

JORDAN RIVER

Mary and Martha's home

Mt. OF OLIVES

Judea

THIS WAY TO EGYPT

JERUSALEM

● BETHANY

BETHLEHEM

JERICHO

John baptizes Jesus.

Jesus born here

DEAD SEA

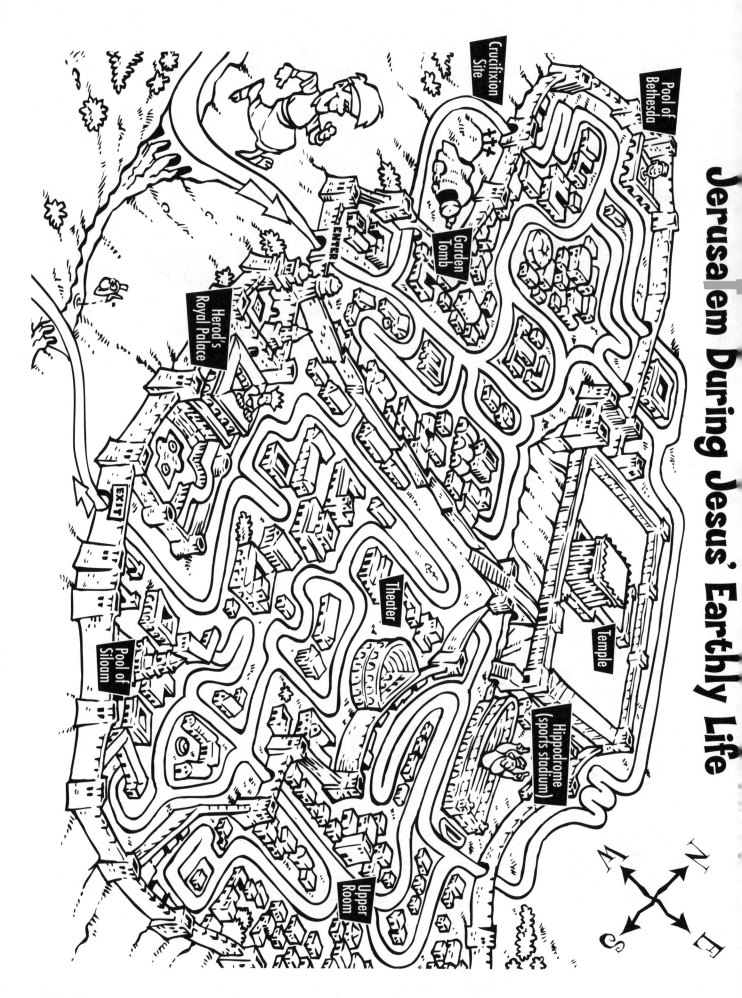

Jerusalem During Jesus' Earthly Life

New Testament Jerusalem

East

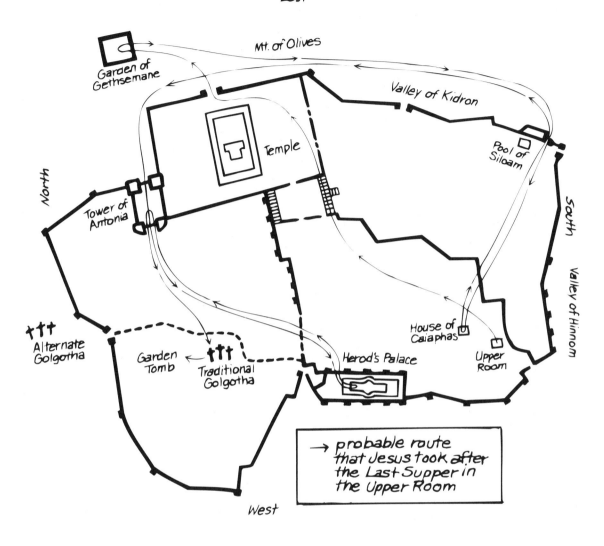

Mt. of Olives

Garden of Gethsemane

Valley of Kidron

Temple

Pool of Siloam

North

Tower of Antonia

South

Valley of Hinnom

✝✝✝
Alternate Golgotha

Garden Tomb

✝✝✝
Traditional Golgotha

House of Caiaphas

Upper Room

Herod's Palace

→ probable route that Jesus took after the Last Supper in the Upper Room

West

Can you find where these events happened?

1. The crowds welcomed Jesus. Matthew 21:9-11

2. Jesus taught. Mark 11:17-19

3. Peter and John prepared the Passover feast. Luke 22:8-13

4. Jesus prayed. Matthew 26:36

5. Jesus was arrested. Matthew 26:36,47-50

6. Jesus was brought before the High Priest. Matthew 26:57,47-58

7. Jesus was crucified. John 19:17,18

8. Jesus was buried. John 19:40-42

9. Jesus rose again. Mark 16:5-8

THE WORLD OF PAUL'S JOURNEYS

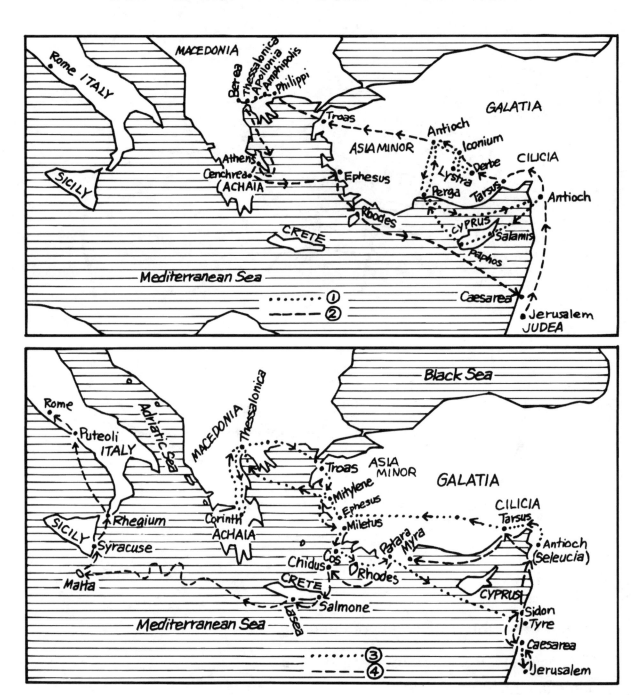

1. Paul's first missionary journey: Acts 13:1—14:28

2. Paul's second missionary journey: Acts 15:36—18:22

3. Paul's third missionary journey: Acts 18:23—21:26

4. Paul's trip to Rome: Acts 21:27—18:31

THE WORLD OF PAUL'S LETTERS

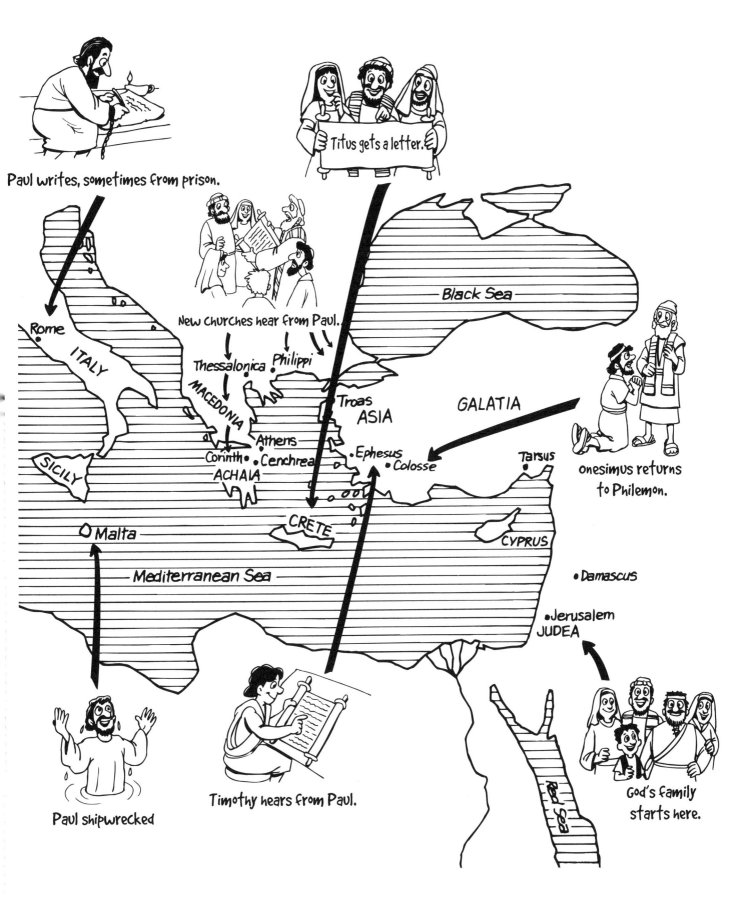

Paul writes, sometimes from prison.

Titus gets a letter.

New churches hear from Paul.

Black Sea

Rome

ITALY

Thessalonica

Philippi

MACEDONIA

Troas

ASIA

GALATIA

Athens

SICILY

Corinth Cenchrea

ACHAIA

Ephesus

Colosse

Tarsus

onesimus returns to Philemon.

CYPRUS

O Malta

CRETE

Mediterranean Sea

Damascus

Jerusalem

JUDEA

Red Sea

God's family starts here.

Paul shipwrecked

Timothy hears from Paul.

WHERE IN THE WORLD?

The Area Where Bible
History Happened

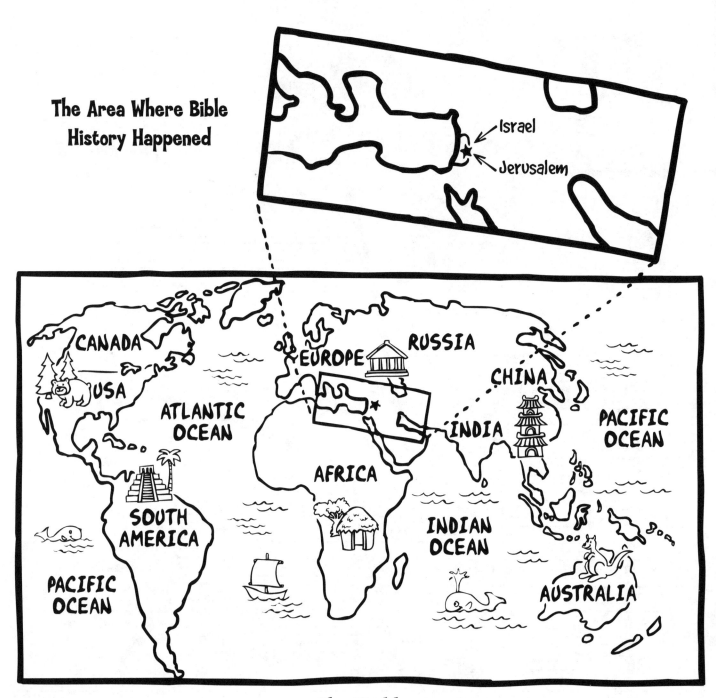

The World

MAP

Lands of the Bible

In your Bible (or a Bible atlas) find a map of Bible lands during the time when Moses led the Hebrew people out of Egypt. Use colored pencils or crayons to label your own map below.

Label and color these bodies of water:
Dead Sea (Salt Sea)
Mediterranean Sea (Great Sea)
Jordan River
Nile River
Red Sea
Sea of Galilee (Sea of Kinnereth)

Label each mountain shown by a triangle:
Mt. Ebal
Mt. Gerizim
Mt. Nebo
Mt. Sinai

Label each city shown by a dot:
Hebron
Jericho
Kadesh Barnea
Rameses

Label and color these areas or countries:
Canaan
Egypt

MAP
Map of Miracles

1. Circle the name of the town where Jesus healed a paralyzed man. (Mark 2:1-12)

2. Draw a square around the name of the sea Jesus calmed. (Luke 8:22-26)

3. Underline the name of the town where Jesus fed 5,000 people with a boy's lunch. (Luke 9:10-17)

4. Draw an *X* by the area where Jesus healed a deaf man. (Mark 7:31-37)

5. Draw a star by the name of the town where Jesus brought a man back to life. (John 11:17-44)

6. Draw a triangle around the name of the town where Jesus changed water into wine. (John 2:1-11)

7. Draw a heart by the name of the town where Jesus healed two blind men. (Matthew 20:29-34)

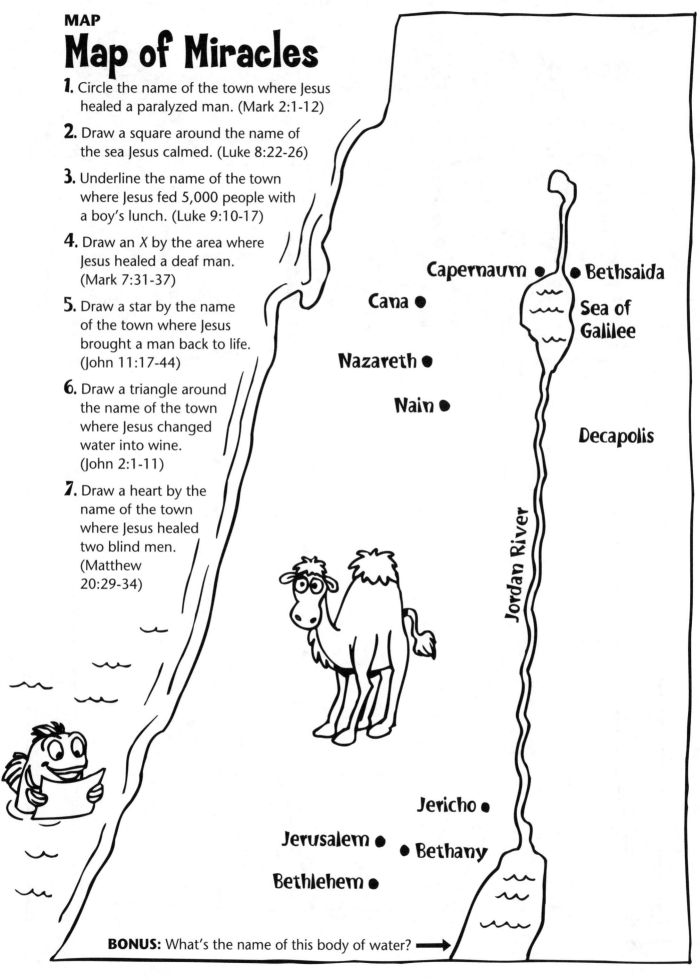

Capernaum •
• Bethsaida
Cana •
Sea of Galilee
Nazareth •
Nain •
Decapolis
Jordan River
Jericho •
Jerusalem •
• Bethany
Bethlehem •

BONUS: What's the name of this body of water? ➞

Paul's Letters

MAP

The apostle Paul wrote letters to Christians who lived in a variety of cities. Read each clue and then find the square on the map where the letter and number meet. Write the name of the city or region in that square. Draw a line from each city or region to the name of Paul's letter.

1. The region of Galatia (B9, B10).
2. The church in Rome (A1).
3. The Christians in Ephesus (C6).
4. The city of Philippi (B5).
5. Paul wrote two letters to the church in Thessalonica (B4).
6. Colossae is in D7.
7. The city of Corinth (C4).

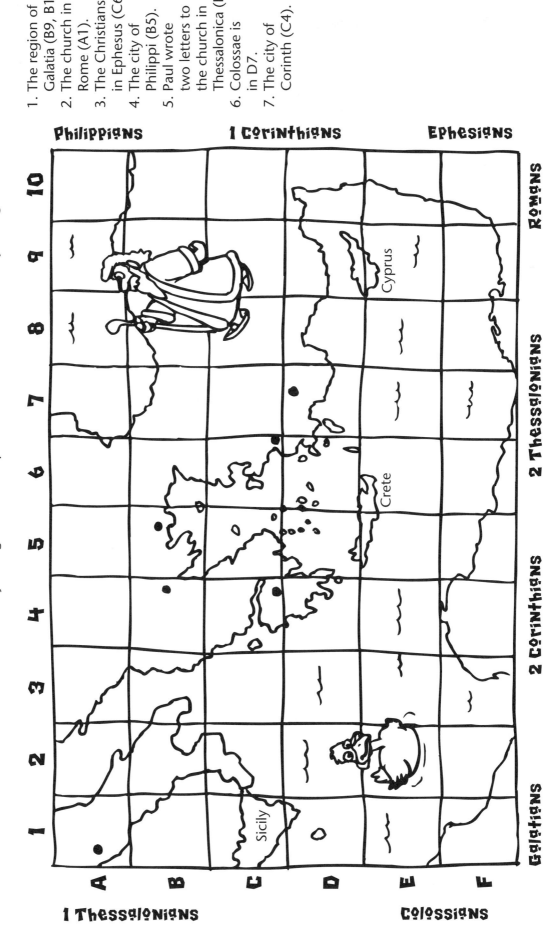

MAP
Lands of the Bible

In your Bible (or a Bible atlas) find a map of Bible lands during the time when Moses led the Hebrew people out of Egypt. Use colored pencils or crayons to label your own map below.

Label and color these bodies of water:
Dead Sea (Salt Sea)
Mediterranean Sea (Great Sea)
Jordan River
Nile River
Red Sea
Sea of Galilee (Sea of Kinnereth)

Label each mountain shown by a triangle:
Mt. Ebal
Mt. Gerizim
Mt. Nebo
Mt. Sinai

Label each city shown by a dot:
Hebron
Jericho
Kadesh Barnea
Rameses

Label and color these areas or countries:
Canaan
Egypt

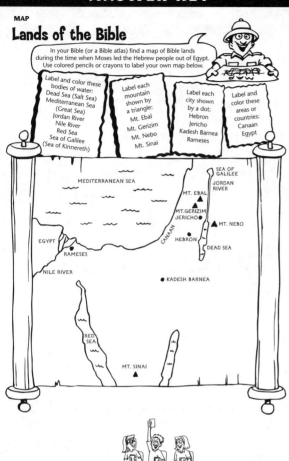

MAP
Map of Miracles

1. Circle the name of the town where Jesus healed a paralyzed man. (Mark 2:1-12)

2. Draw a square around the name of the sea Jesus calmed. (Luke 8:22-26)

3. Underline the name of the town where Jesus fed 5,000 people with a boy's lunch. (Luke 9:10-17)

4. Draw an X by the area where Jesus healed a deaf man. (Mark 7:31-37)

5. Draw a star by the name of the town where Jesus brought a man back to life. (John 11:17-44)

6. Draw a triangle around the name of the town where Jesus changed water into wine. (John 2:1-11)

7. Draw a heart by the name of the town where Jesus healed two blind men. (Matthew 20:29-34)

BONUS: What's the name of this body of water? →

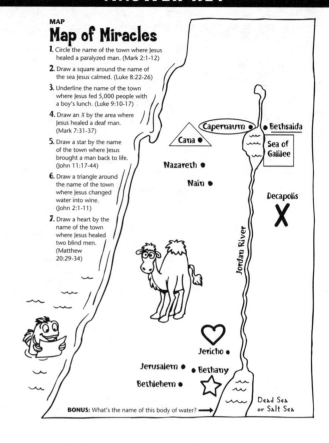

MAP
Paul's Letters

The apostle Paul wrote letters to Christians who lived in a variety of cities. Read each clue and then find the square on the map where the letter and number meet. Write the name of the city or region in that square. Draw a line from each city or region to the name of Paul's letter.

1. The region of Galatia (B9, B10).
2. The church in Rome (A1).
3. The Christians in Ephesus (C6).
4. The city of Philippi (B5).
5. Paul wrote two letters to the church in Thessalonica (B4).
6. Colossae is in D7.
7. The city of Corinth (C4).

122

© 2005 Gospel Light. Permission to photocopy granted. *The Big Book of Bible Facts and Fun*

Built for the Bible

A look at 4 amazing structures that were built as part of God's story!

To help you understand Bible stories better!

Noah's Ark

The Tower of Babel

The Tabernacle

The Temple

NOAH'S ARK

The ark God told Noah to build was 300 cubits long, 50 cubits wide and 30 cubits high.

Was there really room for all those animals?

A cubit is the distance from a man's elbow to the tip of his longest finger. (Today's "standard cubit" is 18 inches.) So how big was the ark in feet?* In meters?**

Consider this: Noah's ark was about the size of one and one-half football fields or two Boeing 747s. It held about as much as 569 railroad stock cars.

That's BIG!

The ark was waterproofed by filling in every crack with pitch (a tar-like substance) both inside and out.

You bet it floated!

The ark held Noah, his family and every kind of animal that couldn't survive in the water.

*450 feet long, 75 feet wide and 45 feet high. ** 137.16 meters long, 22.86 meters wide, 13.71 meters high.

THE TOWER OF BABEL

How many languages do you speak?
How many languages can you think of?

The ruin of a ziggurat (ZIG ur ot) at Nimrud (in modern Iraq) is traditionally called the Tower of Babel.

Most ziggurats were made of mud and straw bricks. The bricks were baked to make them stronger. They were held together with asphalt or tar.

The people began to build a tower they thought would show how powerful they were. They planned for their tower to reach to heaven!

But God had other plans. He changed their one language into many languages. When people couldn't understand each other, they couldn't work together! People who spoke the same language began to live together and then moved to other areas.

THE TABERNACLE

When God's people left Egypt for Canaan, they lived in tents—and moved often! During this time, God gave them instructions for making a place to worship Him—a very special tent called the Tabernacle. (See Exodus 25—27:21.)

God gave detailed instructions for how to make each and every part of the Tabernacle. He gave specific instructions about how to make its furniture. He also gave instructions for how the priests were to dress.

The Tabernacle was in use until Solomon built the first Temple.

THE FURNITURE

The Temple used these same furnishings.

TABLE (gold-covered, solid gold implements) held 12 loaves of bread that stood for the 12 tribes of God's people.

ARK OF THE COVENANT (gold-covered box, solid gold top) held items that reminded the people of God's promises. God's presence stayed with the Ark.

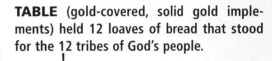

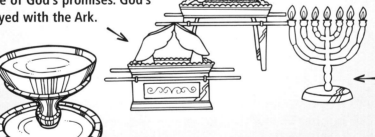

LAMP STAND (solid gold) stayed lit all of the time.

BASIN (bronze) was for washing. (Remember, there was no running water!)

INCENSE ALTAR (gold-covered wood) was where priests burned good-smelling incense.

ALTAR OF SACRIFICE (bronze-covered wood) was where priests offered animal sacrifices.

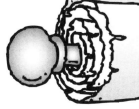

THE TEMPLE

The first Temple was built during the time of King Solomon. It was a permanent building where God's people could come to worship Him.

Over years and years, the people would worship at the Temple, but then they would disobey God and worship idols. Then God would send trouble and they would remember they needed to worship God.

Some kings obeyed God, got rid of the idols and repaired the Temple. Some kings just began more worship of false gods!

When the Babylonians attacked, they also destroyed Solomon's Temple. But when God's people returned 70 years later, they began to build the **Second Temple**.

Herod's Temple (in Jesus' day) was built over and around the Second Temple but was destroyed by the Romans in A.D. 70.

The Israelites disobeyed God.

God sent help.

The Israelites prayed to God for help.

God allowed their enemies to make life hard for them.

Who's Who in the Bible

In Earth's Most Amazing Book, it's one BIG family!

Information pages that give an overview of some Bible people, along with puzzle pages about Bible people. Also, highlights of Bible history presented in a simplified, reproducible time line of Bible people and events to know.

Jesus' Family Tree

(The Way Back Tree!)

Adam
Eve

Abraham

Ruth
Boaz

David

Mary
(Joseph was also a
descendant of David!)

Jesus

The Gospels of Matthew and Luke trace Jesus' family tree
through King David back to Abraham and Adam.

You can read all of the details there!

The Disciples

There were 12. But who were they?

What are their names again?

Andrew and **Simon** were brothers and former fishermen. Andrew brought Simon to meet Jesus. Jesus named Simon "Peter," or "rock."

James was also called **James the younger**, or James, Alphaeus' son.

Judas Iscariot kept the money-bag and betrayed Jesus. He was replaced by Matthias.

Bartholomew was also called **Nathanael**. When Jesus told him He had seen him under a fig tree before they had ever met, Bart/Nate decided right then that Jesus is the Son of God!

Simon was also called **Simon the Zealot**, possibly because he'd been part of the political party of the Zealots, who wanted to drive the Romans out of Israel.

Matthew, also called **Levi**, was a former tax collector and the author of the first book of the New Testament.

Judas (whose father's name was James) was also called **Thaddeus**.

James and **John** were also brothers and former fishermen. They were Zebedee's sons. John wrote the Gospel of John and 3 other letters in the New Testament.

Thomas, also called **Didymus** (twin), couldn't believe Jesus was alive until he saw and touched Him.

Philip (who knew how much it would cost to feed the crowd in John 5) is not the same Philip as the deacon in Acts 6 who later talked with the Ethiopian.

BIBLE CHARACTERS— OLD TESTAMENT

WHO'S WHO?

Complete the puzzle by reading the Bible verses and filling in the names of these famous Bible characters in the first two books of the Old Testament.

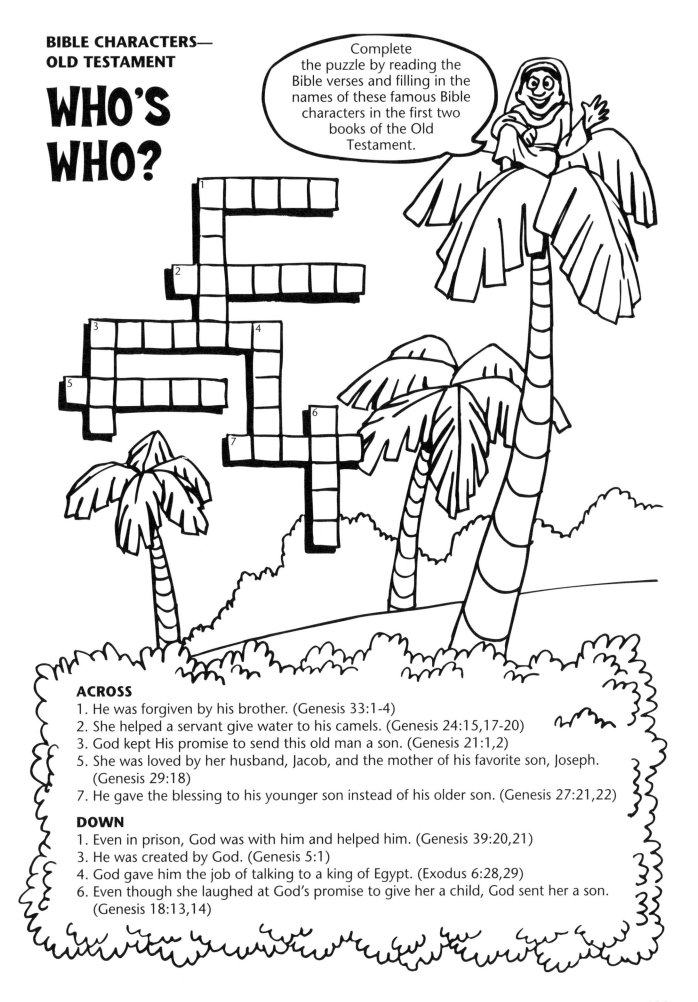

ACROSS
1. He was forgiven by his brother. (Genesis 33:1-4)
2. She helped a servant give water to his camels. (Genesis 24:15,17-20)
3. God kept His promise to send this old man a son. (Genesis 21:1,2)
5. She was loved by her husband, Jacob, and the mother of his favorite son, Joseph. (Genesis 29:18)
7. He gave the blessing to his younger son instead of his older son. (Genesis 27:21,22)

DOWN
1. Even in prison, God was with him and helped him. (Genesis 39:20,21)
3. He was created by God. (Genesis 5:1)
4. God gave him the job of talking to a king of Egypt. (Exodus 6:28,29)
6. Even though she laughed at God's promise to give her a child, God sent her a son. (Genesis 18:13,14)

KING QUIZ

Read the Bible verses to find the missing letters in the names of some of the most famous Bible kings. Then find the names of all these kings in the word search.

These men were kings between 930 BC and 415 BC.

Ah__ __ (1 Kings 16:33)

Ahaz

Amaziah

Asa

Baasha

__a__id (2 Samuel 2:4)

He__ek__ __h (2 Kings 18:16)

Hoshea

Jehoahaz

Jehoash

Jehoiakim

Jehoram

Jehoshaphat

J__ __u (2 Kings 9:5,6)

__er__b__am (1 Kings 12:20)

Jo__i__h (2 Kings 23:23)

Jotham

M__na__ __eh (2 Kings 21:1)

Menahem

Omri

Pekah

__eh__b__am (1 Kings 11:43)

S__u __ (1 Samuel 11:15)

S__lo__o__ (1 Kings 1:39)

Uzziah

Zedekiah

```
                      B
                   C  A  T
      I  J  Y   O  I  A  M  U      P  K  T
      T  E  S  C  B  R  S  B  D   S  R  D  G
S  M     K  H  O  F  N  K  M  H  A  S  P  T  L  Z  O        K  I
D  L  R  G  A  O  L  J  E  H  O  A  H  A  Z  G  O  P  R  Q  V  J  T
B  J  P  J  Z  I  O  E  H  Q  L  U  A  S  N  D  E  X  L  D  A  E  U
D  S  O  E  B  A  M  H  E  M  P  S  L  A  H  A  Z  C  B  R  M  R  W
F  V  N  H  U  K  O  O  M  A  E  H  S  O  H  V  R  F  Q  E  A  O  Y
H  I  R  U  A  I  N  R  I  N  K  D  J  O  S  I  A  H  A  H  Z  B  C
J  B  T  B  H  M  R  A  A  A  Y  O  O  P  D  V  W  R  O  I  O  E
L  H  L  B  A  T  P  M  H  S  H  B  A  R  T  I  X  L  I  B  A  A  G
N  Y  D  A  I  K  B  U  N  S  V  L  S  Y  W  H  O  Z  K  O  H  M  I
P  L  V  B  Z  T  E  C  F  E  J  E  H  O  S  H  A  P  H  A  T  S  K
R  N  H  E  Z  E  K  I  A  H  N  M  E  N  A  H  E  M  U  M  O  I  M
T  C  P  L  U  J  E  H  O  A  S  H  H  A  I  K  E  D  E  Z  Q  G  O
```

BIBLE CHARACTERS—WOMEN
Name That Maze

Draw a line to show the correct path through this maze. The letters along the correct path form the names of women we read about in the Bible.

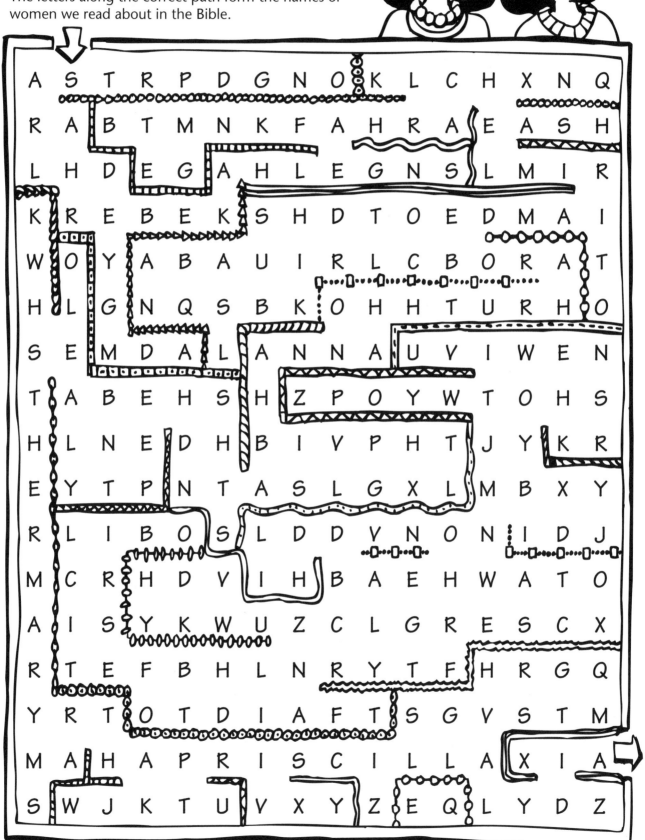

Puzzling Names

Read the Bible verses and fill in the names
of these famous people from the book of Acts.

ACROSS
1. He preached about Jesus
   to a large crowd in Jerusalem.
   (Acts 2:14)
2. She lived in Philippi and became
   a Christian after listening to Paul
   tell about Jesus. (Acts 16:14)
5. The Bible describes this man as so full
   of God's power that he was able to do
   many miracles. Later, he was killed
   because of his faith in God. (Acts 6:8)

DOWN
1. After he believed that
   Jesus is God's Son, this man
   traveled to many places telling
   about Jesus. (Acts 17:2,3)
3. She was known for helping
   poor widows. (Acts 9:36)
4. This man wrote five books of the
   New Testament. Four of these
   books are named after him.
6. He explained the Scriptures to an
   Ethiopian (Acts 8:26,27,35)

BIBLE CHARACTERS—OLD TESTAMENT

WHO'S WHO?

Complete the puzzle by reading the Bible verses and filling in the names of these famous Bible characters in the first two books of the Old Testament.

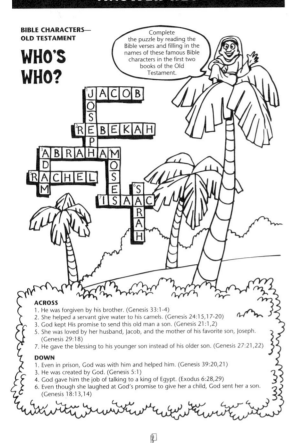

Crossword answers:
JACOB, JOSEPH, REBEKAH, ABRAHAM, ADAM, MOSES, RACHEL, ISAAC, SARAH

ACROSS
1. He was forgiven by his brother. (Genesis 33:1-4)
2. She helped a servant give water to his camels. (Genesis 24:15,17-20)
3. God kept His promise to send this old man a son. (Genesis 21:1,2)
5. She was loved by her husband, Jacob, and the mother of his favorite son, Joseph. (Genesis 29:18)
7. He gave the blessing to his younger son instead of his older son. (Genesis 27:21,22)

DOWN
1. Even in prison, God was with him and helped him. (Genesis 39:20,21)
3. He was created by God. (Genesis 5:1)
4. God gave him the job of talking to a king of Egypt. (Exodus 6:28,29)
6. Even though she laughed at God's promise to give her a child, God sent her a son. (Genesis 18:13,14)

BIBLE CHARACTERS—KINGS

KING QUIZ

Read the Bible verses to find the missing letters in the names of some of the most famous Bible kings. Then find the names of all these kings in the word search.

These men were kings between 930 BC and 415 BC.

Ah **a b** (1 Kings 16:33)
Ahaz
Amaziah
Asa
Baasha
D a v id (2 Samuel 2:4)
He **z** ek **i a** h (2 Kings 18:16)
Hoshea
Jehoahaz
Jehoash
Jehoiakim
Jehoram
Jehoshaphat

J e h u (2 Kings 9:5,6)
J ero **b o** am (1 Kings 12:20)
Jo **s i a** h (2 Kings 23:23)
Jotham
M **a** na **s s** eh (2 Kings 21:1)
Menahem
Omri
Pekah
R eh **ob o** am (1 Kings 11:43)
S **a u l** (1 Samuel 11:15)
S **o lo m o** n (1 Kings 1:39)
Uzziah
Zedekiah

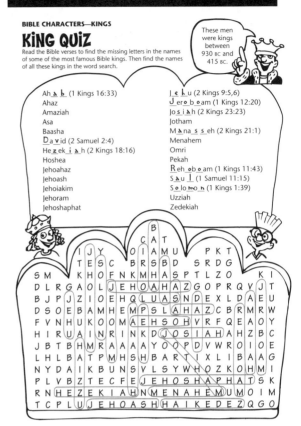

BIBLE CHARACTERS—WOMEN

Name That Maze

Draw a line to show the correct path through this maze. The letters along the correct path form the names of women we read about in the Bible.

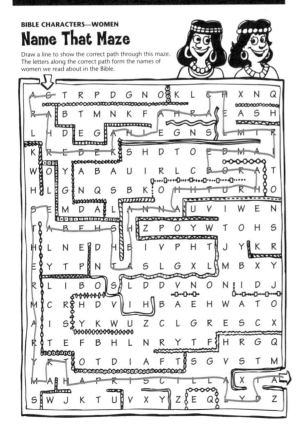

BIBLE CHARACTERS—NEW TESTAMENT

Puzzling Names

Read the Bible verses and fill in the names of these famous people from the book of Acts.

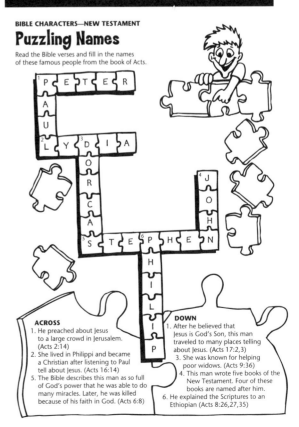

Crossword answers:
PETER, PAUL, LYDIA, DORCAS, JOHN, STEPHEN, PHILIP

ACROSS
1. He preached about Jesus to a large crowd in Jerusalem. (Acts 2:14)
2. She lived in Philippi and became a Christian after listening to Paul tell about Jesus. (Acts 16:14)
5. The Bible describes this man as so full of God's power that he was able to do many miracles. Later, he was killed because of his faith in God. (Acts 6:8)

DOWN
1. After he believed that Jesus is God's Son, this man traveled to many places telling about Jesus. (Acts 17:2,3)
3. She was known for helping poor widows. (Acts 9:36)
4. This man wrote five books of the New Testament. Four of these books are named after him.
6. He explained the Scriptures to an Ethiopian (Acts 8:26,27,35)

BIBLE PEOPLE AND EVENTS TO KNOW TIME LINE

How to Use the Time Line

1. Photocopy each page.

2. Using a paper cutter or scissors, cut each page in half.

3. Invite students to color time line art.

4. Line up each page so that the black lines on the outside edges of the time line are connected and in correct order. Trim and tape as desired.

5. If desired, laminate or cover the finished time line with clear Con-Tact paper.

6. Post on a classroom wall at students' eye level as an easy-to-use reference.

Bible People and Events to Know

NOTE: All dates are approximate.

IN THE BEGINNING GOD CREATED THE HEAVENS AND THE EARTH.

Adam and Eve disobey God.

God floods the Earth.

People build a tower; God confuses their language.

2100 B.C.

Abraham travels to Canaan.

Isaac born to Abraham and Sarah

Jacob and Esau born to Isaac and Rebekah

1900 B.C.

Jacob's son Joseph a slave in Egypt

1850 B.C.

Joseph brings his family to Egypt.

Israel lives in Egypt; slavery

God calls Moses to lead Israel.

1450 B.C.

Israel escapes from Egypt.

Joshua and Caleb tell about the good land of Canaan.

40 years traveling in the desert

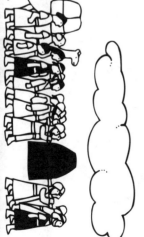

The Tabernacle is built.

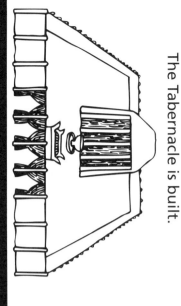

Rahab helps the spies.

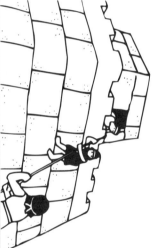

The Israelites cross the Jordan into Canaan.

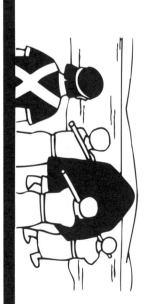

1400 B.C. Time of Settlement

God makes Jericho's walls fall.

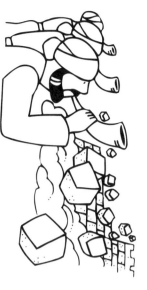

Joshua divides the land.

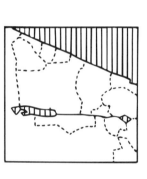

Joshua dies.

Ruth marries Boaz.

Deborah and Barak defeat an army.

Gideon defeats an army.

Samson defeats the Philistines.

Samuel is brought to the Tabernacle.

Samuel leads Israel.

1050 B.C.–600 B.C. Time of the Kings

Saul becomes the first king.

Samuel anoints David as next king.

David defeats Goliath.

David and Jonathan are friends.

1010 B.C.

Saul tries to kill David.

David becomes king.

God's Ark comes to Jerusalem.

970 B.C.

Solomon becomes third king.

The Temple is built in Jerusalem.

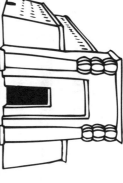
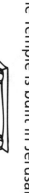

Solomon listens to his wives and begins to worship idols.

The kingdom divides into Israel and Judah.

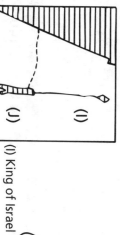

(I)

(J)

(I) King of Israel
(J) King of Judah

The people worship idols.

870 B.C.

Elijah's contest shows the one true God.

Elijah trains Elisha.

Elijah goes to heaven.

840 B.C.   (I) King of Israel   (J) King of Judah   830 B.C.

Jehu (I)

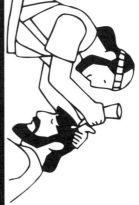

Joash (J)

Joash rebuilds the Temple.

790 B.C.

Prophets: Jonah (Nineveh), Amos (I), Hosea (I), Isaiah (J), Micah (J)

Kings: Jeroboam 2 (I), Uzziah (J), Jotham (J), Pekah (I), Hoshea (I), Ahaz (J)

(J) King of Judah   (I) King of Israel

722 B.C.

Israel (northern kingdom) taken captive to Assyria

MORE KINGS AND PROPHETS

Prophet Jeremiah (J)

King Jehoiakim (J)

605-586 B.C.

Many captives from Judah taken to Babylon; Jerusalem destroyed

540 B.C.

King Cyrus decrees that the people of Judah may return home.

Many people return to Judah.

444 B.C.

Nehemiah leads a rebuilding of Jerusalem's walls.

4OO YEARS BETWEEN THE OLD AND NEW TESTAMENTS

(B.C.* becomes A.D.**)

Jesus is born.

Jesus baptized by John

Jesus begins healing many.

A.D. 26

* B.C. = **Before Christ**   ** A.D.= **Anno Domini, or "in the year of our Lord"**

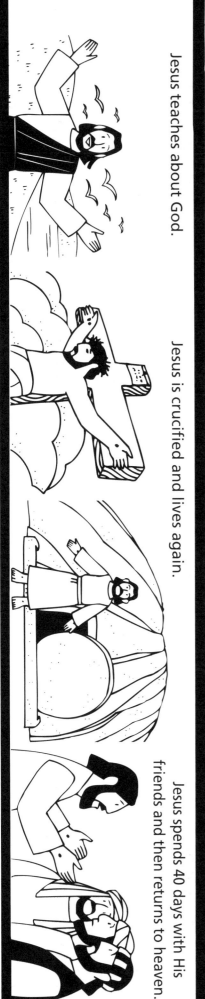

Jesus teaches about God.

Jesus is crucified and lives again.

A.D. 29

Jesus spends 40 days with His friends and then returns to heaven.

A.D. 30

The Holy Spirit comes to Jesus' followers.

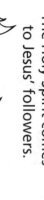

A.D. 35

Jesus' followers are persecuted.

Saul meets Jesus.

A.D. 45-53

Saul becomes Paul and travels . . .

. . . to tell the good news about Jesus.

A.D. 60

Paul a prisoner in Rome

A.D. 90

John writes the final book of the Bible.

Bible Times Coloring Pages

Pages to color that illustrate aspects of life in Bible times.

ARCHAEOLOGISTS AFOOT!

The archaeologists at this dig are busy learning about life in Bible times. How many of these activities can you find in the picture?

Word Box	Digging	Washing	Sifting	Moving dirt	Uncovering bones	Inspecting a find
	Mapping (gridding) an area		Photographing	Drawing	Brushing	Removing tiles

BEDS

CELEBRATION

CHORES

Clothing

EATING

GAMES

HOUSES

MARKETPLACE

How many things for sale can you count? How many different jobs are people doing in the marketplace?

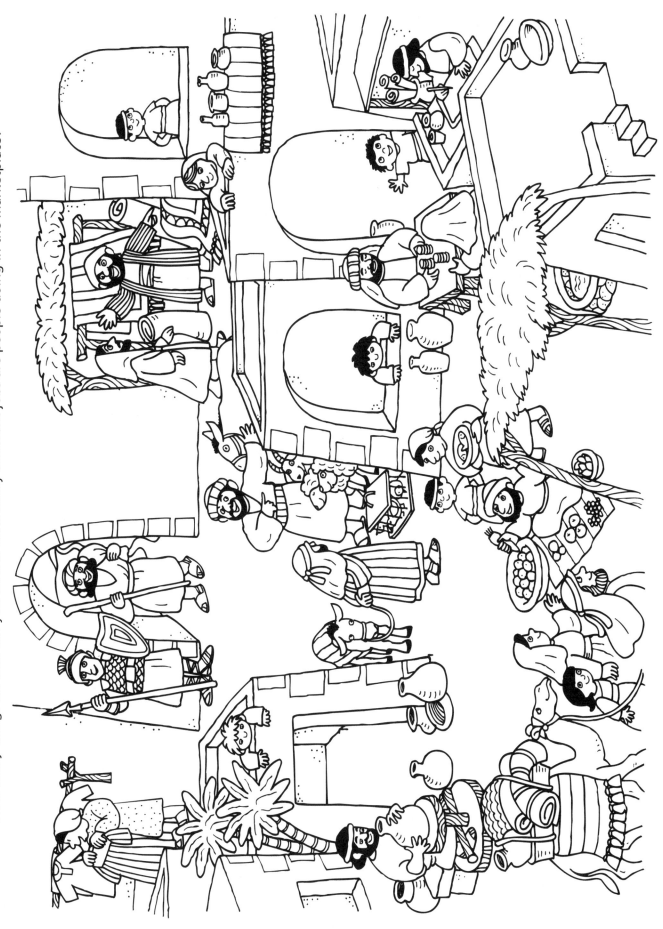

Outdoor Life

Praise

READING GOD'S WORD

© 2005 Gospel Light. Permission to photocopy granted. *The Big Book of Bible Facts and Fun*

School

SCROLLS

SHEPHERD

TENTS

TRAVEL

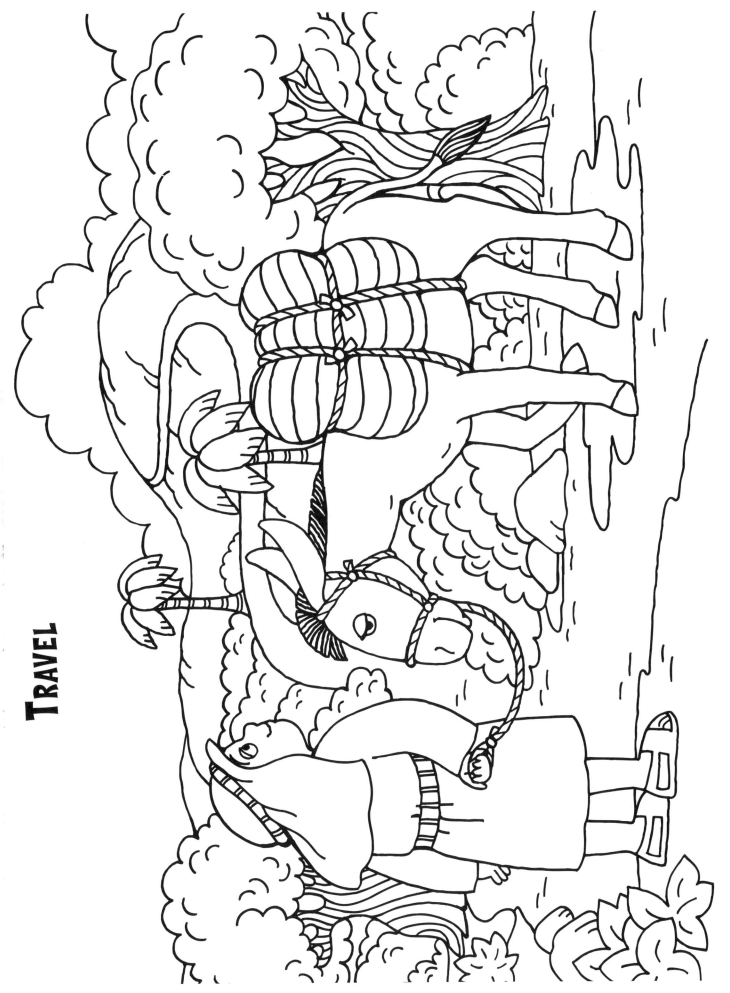

WEAVING

Bible Dictionary

A Bible dictionary to help you with studying God's Word on your own!

A simplified Bible Dictionary to help students understand aspects of the Bible. Also includes puzzles solved by using a Bible Dictionary.

Abba (ab-uh)

An Aramaic word that means "Daddy." Aramaic was the language spoken by Jesus and other Jews living in Israel.

adultery (uh-DUL-ter-ee)

Sexual union between a man and a woman when either of them is married to someone else. *Adultery* is a sin.

adversary (AD-vuh-sair-ee)

An enemy or someone who is against you.

advocate (AD-vuh-kit)

Someone who supports, comforts, gives help or speaks up for another person. Jesus and the Holy Spirit are *Advocates* for members of God's family.

affliction (uh-FLICK-shun)

Great trouble or pain.

alien (AYL-yun or AY-lee-en)

A person from another country; a foreigner.

altar (AWL-ter)

A place where sacrifices were made to worship God. An *altar* could be a pile of dirt or stones, a raised platform of wood, marble, metal or other materials.

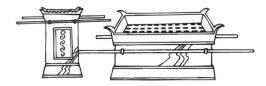

amen (ay-MEN or ah-MEN)

"Let it be so!" or "This is the truth!" *Amen* is often said after a prayer to show that people agree with what has been said and believe that it will happen.

Ancient of Days

A name for God that describes Him as the everlasting ruler of heaven and Earth.

angels (AYN-juls)

Heavenly beings created by God before He created Adam and Eve. *Angels* act as God's messengers to men and women. They also worship God.

anoint (uh-NOINT)

To pour oil on a person or thing. A person was *anointed* to show that God had chosen him or her to do a special job. Samuel *anointed* David to show God had chosen him to be king.

antichrist (AN-tih-christ)

A great enemy of Christ Jesus who pretends to be the Messiah. The Bible tells us that before the second coming of Christ, an *antichrist* will rule over the world.

apostle (uh-PAH-sul)

A person chosen and sent out as a messenger. In the New Testament, *apostle* usually refers to one of the 12 men Jesus chose to be His special disciples. Paul and some other leaders in the Early Church were also called *apostles*.

appeal to Caesar (SEE-zer)

If a Roman citizen accused of a crime felt that the trial or verdict was unfair, he could request that the emperor (Caesar) hear the case. Paul, a Roman citizen, once did this.

ark of God or **ark of the covenant**

A special wooden chest that was covered with gold. God told Moses exactly how to make the *ark* because it was to show the people of Israel that God was with them. The *ark* was about 4 feet (1.2 m) long, 2½ feet (.8 m) tall and 2½ feet (.8 m) wide. On top, two golden figures of angels faced each other. The two tables of stone on which the Ten Commandments were written, a pot of manna, and Aaron's rod that had budded were kept inside the *ark*. The *ark* was placed in the most holy place in the Tabernacle.

Aramaic (air-uh-MAY-ik)

The main language spoken by Jesus and other people who lived in Israel when Jesus lived on Earth.

armor-bearer (ARE-mur-BARE-ur)

A person who carried the large shield and necessary weapons for a king or an army officer.

archangel (ARK-ayn-jul)

A leader of other angels; the highest rank among angels.

Artemis (AR-tuh-mis)

A Greek goddess whose Roman name was Diana. Her most beautiful temple was built in Ephesus.

ascend (uh-SEND)

To go up. Jesus *ascended* to heaven to return to God the Father. Since Jerusalem is on a hill, the Bible also talks about God's people *ascending* to Jerusalem.

atonement (uh-TONE-ment)

To make up for a wrong act; to become friends again. In the Bible, *atonement* usually means to become friends with God after sin has separated us from Him. In the Old Testament, the Israelites brought sacrifices to *atone* for their sins. The New Testament teaches that Jesus Christ made *atonement* for our sins when He died on the cross. Because Jesus died to "make up" for our sins, we can have peace with God.

Baal (bale)

The name *Baal* means "master." 1. The name of many false gods worshiped by the people of Canaan. They thought the *Baal* gods ruled their land, crops and animals. 2. Place name combined with the name *Baal*, such as *Baal*-Hermon, showed that Hermon belonged to *Baal*. When the Israelites came to the Promised Land, each area of the land had its own *Baal* god. 3. Later, *Baal* became the name for the chief male god of the Canaanites who was believed to bring sun and rain and make crops grow. The Israelites were often tempted to worship *Baal*—something God had told them they were never to do.

balm (bawm)

A sticky, sweet-smelling sap used as a medicine to heal sores or relieve pain. The plant or tree from which the sap was taken is unknown today.

balsam trees (BOL-sum)

Trees that grow in the Jericho Plain. The sweet-smelling sap of the trees and the oil from their fruit were used as medicine.

baptize (BAP-tize)

In the Old Testament, to *baptize* meant to wash with water. But in the New Testament, when John the Baptist called the people to be *baptized*, he was using water to show that people were truly sorry for the wrong things they had done and that they were asking God to forgive their sins. Today, a person is *baptized* to show that he or she is a member of God's family.

barren (BEAR-un) A woman who could not have children was called *barren*. Fields that did not produce crops or fruit trees that did not grow fruit were also called *barren*.

Beelzebub (bee-EL-zee-bub)

A god the Philistines worshiped. In the New Testament, *Beelzebub* (or Beelzebul) is another name for Satan, the prince of the demons.

believe

To have faith or to trust that something is true. The Bible tells us that we can *believe* that Jesus Christ is God's Son and trust Him to keep His promise to forgive our sins. We show that we *believe* that God loves us and wants what is best for us by obeying His commands.

betrothed (be-TROTHT)

Engaged to be married. Mary was *betrothed* to Joseph before they were married.

bier (beer)

A stretcher or platform on which a dead body was carried to the place where it would be buried.

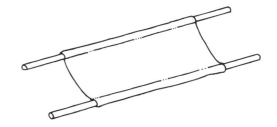

birthright (BURTH-rite)

The special rights the oldest son in a Hebrew family enjoyed. When his father died, the oldest son received a double share of all that his father owned. He also received the right to make decisions for the entire family. Esau sold his *birthright* to Jacob for a bowl of stew.

bitter herbs (urbs)

A bitter-tasting green salad eaten at Passover to remind the Israelites of the sorrow, pain and *bitter* hardships their ancestors suffered as slaves in Egypt.

blaspheme (BLAS-feem)

1. To say bad things against God. 2. To swear using God's name. 3. To do actions that show disrespect to God. The Bible says that *blasphemy* is a sin. The Jews punished *blasphemers* by stoning them to death. Jesus and Stephen were falsely accused of *blasphemy*.

blemish (BLEM-ish)

A defect, spot or mark that makes something not perfect. In Old Testament times, a lamb offered as a sacrifice had to be without any *blemish*.

bless

1. To ask God to do good things for another person. 2. To praise, worship and thank God. 3. To give good things or to show kindness to another. The Bible says that God *blesses* all people by giving them many good things and showing great kindness to them.

bondage (BON-dij)

Being in slavery. In the Old Testament, the Israelites were in *bondage* to the Egyptians for many years. In the New Testament, *bondage* means slavery to sin. Jesus died and rose again to set people free from sin. Christians are no longer slaves in *bondage* to sin, but are free to love and obey God and His Son, Jesus.

breastpiece or **breastplate**

1. A square of colored linen cloth worn by the high priest when he entered the Holy Place. The *breastpiece* was decorated with 12 precious stones. Each stone represented one of the 12 tribes of Israel. The *breastpiece* reminded the priest to pray for each of the tribes of Israel. 2. A piece of metal armor that protected a soldier's throat and chest.

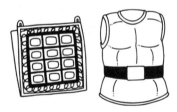

burnt offering (OFF-ring)

A sacrifice, or gift, to God that was burned on an altar. The offering was a perfect animal, such as a goat, sheep, lamb or ram. *Burnt offerings* were always given for cleansing, or atonement, for sin.

Caesar (SEE-zer)

The family name of Julius Caesar, a famous Roman leader. Later the name *Caesar* was added to the name of each Roman ruler, so it became a title that meant the same as "emperor" or "king."

capstone (KAP-stone)

The final, most important stone that finishes a wall. When the Bible calls Jesus a *capstone*, it reminds us that He is the head of the Church and that He holds all Christians together.

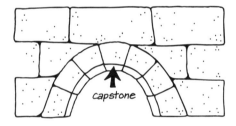

capstone

caravan (CARE-uh-van)

A group of people (with their belongings) who travel together for protection from robbers and wild animals. In Bible times, families often traveled in *caravans*. Traders also traveled in *caravans*.

census (SEN-sus)

The counting of the number of people living in an area or country.

centurion (sen-TOUR-ee-un)

An officer in the Roman army who was the leader of 80-100 men.

chaff

The worthless husks removed from grain. Farmers in Bible times got rid of *chaff* by throwing grain into the air on windy days. The light *chaff* blew away on the wind; the heavier grain fell to the ground. In the Bible, the word *chaff* often means something bad or worthless.

chariot (CHAIR-ee-ut)

An open, two- or four-wheeled cart pulled by horses.

chief priest

See *high priest*.

Christ

The Greek word that means "Chosen One." "Messiah" is the Hebrew word meaning the same thing. Jesus is the *Christ*.

This is my Son, whom I love.

Christian (KRIS-chun)

In the Bible, the word meant "Christ's person" or "little Christ." Today people who believe Jesus Christ is God's Son and follow His teachings are called *Christians*.

Circumcise (SIR-cum-size)

To cut an unneeded flap of skin, called the foreskin, from the penis. For the Israelites, *circumcision* was a sign of the special agreement (or covenant) they had with God: If they worshiped and obeyed Him, He would be their God and they would be His people. Abraham was the first Hebrew to be *circumcised*. After Abraham, Hebrew baby boys were *circumcised* when they were eight days old. Leaders in the Early Church said that it was not necessary for men or boys to be *circumcised* to become part of God's family.

cistern (SIS-turn)

A hole dug in the earth or a rock to collect and store water. Empty *cisterns* were sometimes used as prisons or places to store grain.

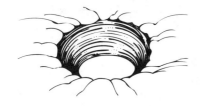

City of David

1. Another name for the town of Bethlehem where *David* was born. 2. Part of the city of Jerusalem was known as the *City of David*. 3. The entire walled city of Jerusalem is also sometimes called the *City of David*.

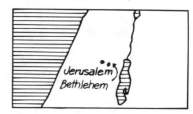

Jerusalem
Bethlehem

city of refuge (REF-yooj)

One of six cities set aside by Moses where a person who had accidentally killed someone could stay until a fair trial could be held. While the person was in a *city of refuge*, he would be safe from family or friends of the dead person who might want to kill him.

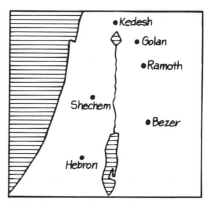

Kedesh
Golan
Ramoth
Shechem
Bezer
Hebron

cloak (kloke)

A long, loose fitting robe people in Bible times wore over their other clothing.

Outer Cloak

commandment (kuh-MAND-ment)

A rule or teaching people are to follow. Moses received the Ten Commandments from God. The Bible gives *commandments* for Christians to follow because they love Him and want to obey His Word.

conceive (kun-SEEV)

1. To become pregnant. 2. To think up or imagine something.

concubine (KON-ku-bine)

A slave woman in Bible times who lived with an Israelite family and had children by the father of the family. She was considered an extra or second-class wife.

condemn (kun-DEM)

1. To find someone guilty of doing something wrong and to declare or pronounce a punishment. 2. To be against or disapprove of something because it is wrong.

confess (kun-FESS)

1. To tell or agree about what is true. 2. *Confess* sometimes means to tell God your sins. 3. *Confess* can also mean to say in front of other people that you believe that Jesus is God's Son and that He died and rose again to forgive you of your sins.

conscience (KON-shuns)

A feeling about what is right and what is wrong; a sense of knowing what is good and what is bad.

consecrate (KON-suh-krate)

To set apart something or someone to serve God in a special way.

convert (KON-vert)

A person who has changed from one belief or way of thinking to another. A person who decides to follow God's way instead of his or her own way has become a *convert*.

cornerstone

A large stone in the foundation of a building at the corner of two walls. It holds the building together. The cornerstone is the first and most important stone laid when a building is started. Jesus is called the *cornerstone* of our faith in God because He is the most important part of our knowing who God is.

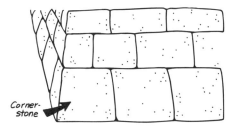

Cornerstone

counselor (KOUN-sel-or) One who gives advice or help. Sometimes the Bible uses the word *Counselor* as another name for Jesus. In the New Testament, the Holy Spirit is also called the *Counselor* of Christians.

covenant (KUV-uh-nunt)

An agreement. Sometimes a *covenant* was made between two people or groups of people. Both sides decided what the agreement would be. However, in the Bible, the word usually refers to an agreement between God and people. In a *covenant* between God and people, God decides what shall be done and the people agree to live by the *covenant*.

covet (KUV-et)

Wanting very much to have something that belongs to someone else.

I wish that was mine.

create (kree-ATE)

To cause something new to exist or to happen. God *created* everything that exists.

crucify (KROO-si-fy)

To nail or tie a person to a cross until he or she is dead. *Crucifixion* was a slow, painful punishment the Romans used for their enemies and the worst criminals.

curse (kurse)

In the Bible, to *curse* does not mean to swear or to use bad language. When a person *cursed* something, he or she wished evil or harm to come to it. When God *cursed* something, He declared judgment on something.

deacon (DEE-kun)

Helpers or servants in the church. In the New Testament, men and women *deacons* were chosen to take care of the needs of people in the church. Today churches give their *deacons* many different jobs to do.

debt (det)

Something a person owes someone else—usually money. In the Lord's Prayer, the word *debt* means sins or wrongdoing. The word *debtor* means those who sin against us.

decree (duh-CREE)

An order or law given by a king or ruler. A *decree* was often read in a public place so that many people would hear the new law.

dedicate (DED-i-kate)

To set apart for a special purpose. In the Bible, the word usually means that a person or thing is given to God to serve Him in a special way.

demon (DEE-mun)

An evil spirit working for Satan (the devil). A *demon*-possessed person was controlled by evil spirits. Jesus ordered evil spirits to come out of many people.

denarius (duh-NAIR-ee-us)

Roman money. A *denarius* was a small silver coin. It was the usual payment for about one day's work.

detest (dee-TEST)

To hate.

devote (dee-VOTE)

To set apart for a special purpose or reason.

disciple (dih-SY-pul)

A person who follows the teachings and example of another. In the New Testament, *disciple* usually refers to a person who believed that Jesus is God's Son and loved and obeyed Him. Sometimes *disciples* means the 12 men Jesus chose to be His special friends and helpers. At other times, it refers to all people who love Jesus and obey His teachings.

edict (EE-dikt)

A written law or order given by a king or ruler.

elder (EL-dur)

1. In the Old Testament, an *elder* was an older man in a family, tribe or town. 2. Also in the Old Testament, one of a group of older men in each town. A town's *elders* made major decisions for the town. 3. In the New Testament, the men of the Sanhedrin (the group that governed the Jewish people) were also called *elders*. 4. In the Early Church, church leaders were often called *elders*.

enmity (EN-muh-tee)

Hatred or bad feelings that make two people or groups enemies.

envy (EN-vee)

A strong feeling of jealousy caused by something someone else has or does well. *Envy* can cause a person to try to make him- or herself better than the other person. The Bible says *envy* is a sin.

eternal (ee-TUR-nal)

Lasting forever; without end. God is *eternal* and members of God's family have *eternal* life.

eunuch (YOU-nuk)

1. *Eunuch* was the title sometimes given to the man who was the most important helper or advisor to a king or queen. 2. A man who

could not have children because his sex organs were damaged or defective.

everlasting

Never-ending; forever.

exile (EG-zyl)

To force someone to leave his or her country and live somewhere else. The Jews were in *exile* in Babylon for 70 years.

faith

1. To be certain about the things we cannot see or to trust someone because of who he or she is. For example, a Christian has *faith* that Jesus is God's Son. 2. "The faith" means the whole message about Jesus Christ—that He is God's Son and that He came to take the punishment for our sin so that we may become members of God's family.

faithful

Always loyal and trustworthy. God is *faithful*. We can always trust Him to do whatever He has promised. We are also to be *faithful* in doing what is right.

famine (FAM-in)

A time when there is not enough food to keep people and animals alive. A *famine* can be caused by a lack of rain, by war, insects that eat crops, or bad storms.

fear

Today, *fear* most often means being afraid of something or someone. However, the Bible often uses the word *fear* to describe the sense of respect or awe that people should have for God because of His greatness and His love.

feasts

1. Dinners, celebrations and banquets are often called *feasts* in the Bible. 2. Jewish religious holidays and celebrations are also called *feasts*.

fellowship (FELL-o-ship)

A time when friends who are interested in the same things come together. In the Bible, *fellowship* often means the friendship Christians share because they love God and His Son, Jesus.

fig

A small, brownish, pear-shaped fruit that grows on trees. *Figs* are plentiful in the Middle East. They can be eaten raw, cooked or dried.

firstborn

The first child born into a family. A *firstborn* son received special rights and power. He became head of the family after his father died and he received twice as much money and property as his brothers.

firstfruits

An offering to God of the first vegetables, fruits and grains the Israelites picked from their fields. The people offered their *firstfruits* to God to thank Him for supplying their food.

flax

A useful plant that was grown in Bible times and is still grown today. The seeds of the plant were pressed to make linseed oil. The fibers of the plant were woven into linen cloth.

flint

A very hard stone that can be sharpened to a fine cutting edge.

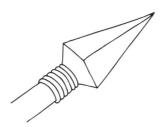

flog

To beat with a whip or stick.

forefather (FOR-father)

A person from whom one is descended; an ancestor. Your father, your grandfather, your great-grandfather and your great-great-grandfather are some of your *forefathers*.

foreigner (FOR-uh-nur)

A person who is from another country.

forgive

To stop feeling angry and to stop blaming a person for something wrong he or she has done; to be friends again. God *forgives* everyone who believes that Jesus died to take the punishment for his or her sins. When

God *forgives* a person, God forgets the person's sins forever. God instructs Christians to *forgive* each other in the same way He has *forgiven* them.

forsake

To leave, to go away from, to leave completely alone.

frankincense (FRANK-in-sense)

A very expensive, hard gum made from the sap of a terebith tree. *Frankincense* was used to make sweet-smelling perfume. The Israelites used *frankincense* in religious ceremonies: One of the special gifts the wise men brought to Jesus was *frankincense*.

Galilee (GAL-uh-lee)

The northern part of Israel in Jesus' day. Jesus grew up, preached and did most of His miracles in *Galilee*. *Galilee* is also the name of a large lake in this area (also called the Sea of Galilee).

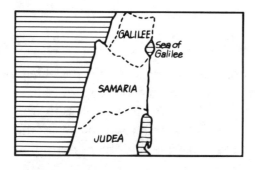

gall (gawl)

A bitter poisonous plant. The juice from the plant may have been used to make a painkiller. Jesus refused a drink of *gall* mixed with wine when He was dying on the cross.

generation (jen-uh-RAY-shun)

All the people born at about the same time. Grandparents, parents and children are three different *generations*.

Gentiles (JEN-tiles)

All people who are not Jewish.

glean (gleen)

To gather leftover fruits or grain that the harvesters missed. The Bible told farmers to leave some crops in the field for hungry people to *glean*.

glory

1. Great beauty, splendor, honor or magnificence that can be seen or sensed. The Israelites

saw the *glory* of the Lord in the cloud that filled the Tabernacle. The shepherds saw the *glory* of the Lord when the angels told them Jesus had been born. 2. *Glory* can also mean to praise, to be happy or to boast.

Golgotha (GAHL-gah-thah)

The place outside Jerusalem where Jesus was hung on a cross. In Aramaic, *Golgotha* means "the place of the skull."

gospel (GOS-pel)

Gospel means "good news." 1. The good news of the Bible that God sent His Son, Jesus, to take the punishment for sin and then raised Him from the dead so that any person who believes may have new life. 2. The story of the life, death and resurrection of Jesus Christ told in the first four books of the New Testament is also called the *gospel*. 3. The first four books of the New Testament, the *Gospels*.

grace

The love and kindness shown to someone who does not deserve it—especially the forgiveness, love and kindness God shows to us. We don't deserve God's *grace* because we sin against Him. God showed *grace* to all people by sending His Son, Jesus, to be our Savior. God's *grace* allows us to become members of His family (see Ephesians 2:8). God's *grace* also keeps on helping us live as God wants us to (see Acts 20:32). A person cannot earn God's *grace* by trying to be good; it is God's free gift.

guilty (GIL-tee)

Having done wrong or broken a law. A person who is *guilty* deserves to be blamed or punished.

Hades (HAY-dees)

A Greek word that means "the place of the dead." Another word used in the Bible that means the same as *Hades* is "Sheol." *Hades* was thought to be a dark, shadowy place. Hell, or Gehenna, was a much more fearful place. It is not the same as *Hades*. If a person has asked Jesus to forgive his or her sins, that person does not need to fear either of these places because he or she will live forever with Jesus.

Hallelujah (HAL-uh-LOO-yuh)

A Hebrew word that means "Praise the Lord!"

harlot

A prostitute; a woman who gets paid for having sexual relations with another person. The Bible says *harlotry* is a sin, but like other sins, it can be forgiven. Sometimes the Bible uses the word *harlot* to describe people who turn away from God to worship idols.

harvest (HAR-vust)

To gather ripe fruits, vegetables, grain and other crops from fields, vineyards and orchards.

Hebrew (HEE-broo)

1. Another name for an Israelite, a member of the nation God chose to be His special people. 2. The language often spoken and written by Israelites. Most of the Old Testament was written in the *Hebrew* language.

heir (air)

A person who has the right to receive the property or position of another person when that person dies. In Bible times, the *heir* was usually a son. The Bible says that anyone who is a member of God's family is His *heir*. God will never die, but because we are His children, God keeps on giving us great love, care and kindness.

herbs (urbs)

Plants or parts of plants used to make teas, medicines and flavorings for food.

Herod (HAIR-ud)

The family name of five kings appointed by the Roman Emperor to rule Israel in New Testament times. Jesus was born during the rule of *Herod* the Great. The names of the other four kings are *Herod* Archelaus, *Herod* Antipas, *Herod* Agrippa I and *Herod* Agrippa II.

high place

Altars and places of worship built on the tops of hills or mountains. Sometimes altars to God were built at *high places*. However, the *high places* were usually for the worship of idols. The Israelites were told to destroy the *high places* in their land where idols were worshiped.

high priest

The most important priest of all the priests who served God in the Tabernacle and later in the Temple. In the Old Testament, the *high priest* offered the most important sacrifices to God for all the people. In New Testament times, he was also a powerful political leader. He was the head of the Sanhedrin—the group of men who governed the Jewish people. He even had a small army. The *high priest* wore the special clothing described in Exodus 28:1-39. Aaron was the first *high priest*. All other *high priests* had to be his descendants.

holy (HO-lee)

1. Perfect and pure. God is *holy*. He is perfect and without sin. Jesus is *holy*, too. He is without sin and dedicated to doing what God wants. Because Jesus died to take the punishment for sin and then rose again, God gives people who believe in Him the power to be *holy*, too. God helps them to become more and more pure and loving, like Jesus. 2. Chosen; set apart; belonging to God. The items made to be used in the Tabernacle and the Temple were *holy*. (People in God's family are *holy* in this way, too.)

Holy Spirit

The personal but unseen power and presence of God in the world. He is the third Person of the trinity. The book of Acts tells us that the *Holy Spirit* came to followers of Jesus in a special way after Jesus had gone back to heaven. The *Holy Spirit* lives within all people who have had their sins forgiven. Jesus said that the *Holy Spirit* is our helper and comforter. The *Holy Spirit* teaches us truth about God. He helps us understand the Bible and helps us pray in the right way. He gives us the power and strength to do what Jesus wants.

Hosanna (hoe-ZAN-uh)

A Hebrew word that means "Save now!" The Hebrews shouted the word to praise someone important.

hypocrite (HIP-uh-krit)

A person who pretends to be something different from what he or she really is. In the Old Testament, *hypocrite* means "a godless person." In the New Testament, it means "a phony." Jesus called the Pharisees *hypocrites* because they did many things to make themselves seem very religious, but they would not listen to God.

idol (eye-dul)

A statue or other image of a god that is made by people and then worshiped as if it had the power of God. Idols are often made of wood, stone or metal. Sometimes, the Bible calls anything that takes the place of God in a person's life an *idol*. God tells us not to worship *idols* but, rather, to worship only Him.

Immanuel (im-MAN-you-el)

A name for Jesus that means "God with us."

incense (IN-sens)

A mixture of spices held together with thick, sticky juice from trees and plants. *Incense* is burned to make a sweet smell. In the Tabernacle and Temple, *incense* was burned on the small, golden *altar of incense* to worship God.

inheritance (in-HAIR-ih-tunce)

Money, property or traditions received from another person. Often, a person receives an *inheritance* after another person's death. The Bible tells us that everything that is God's belongs to Jesus Christ. By His death on the cross, Jesus made it possible for us to share His *inheritance* with Him.

Israel (IZ-ray-el)

1. The special name God gave to Jacob; means "Prince with God."

Israel
(Jacob)

2. Another name for the Hebrew nation—God's chosen people.

Nation of Israel

3. The name *Israel* also means the nation ruled by the judges and the first three Hebrew kings—Saul, David and Solomon.

4. The name given to the northern kingdom after Jeroboam led 10 tribes to separate from Rehoboam and the 2 southern tribes. (The southern kingdom was called Judah.)

5. After the northern kingdom of *Israel* was captured by the Assyrians, the word *Israel* was sometimes used to mean the southern kingdom.

6. It is also a name used for the people of God. The Bible often uses the term "children of *Israel*," meaning they were descendants of Jacob (Israel).

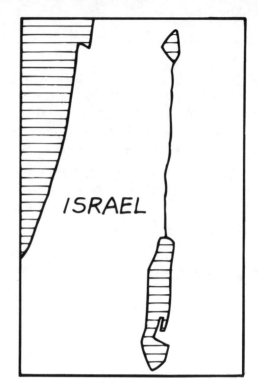

United Kingdom

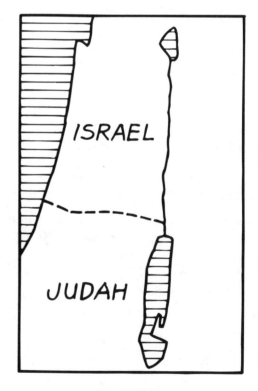

Divided Kingdom

Israelite (IZ-ray-e-lite)

A citizen of the country of *Israel*; a descendant of Jacob (*Israel*).

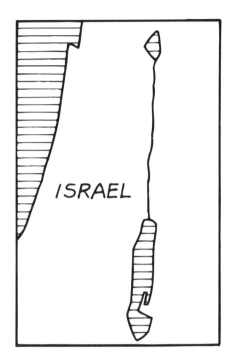

Israelites

Descendants of *Israel* (another name for Jacob). Also called "children of *Israel*."

jealous (JELL-us)

1. Careful to guard and keep safe what one has. This is the kind of *jealousy* the Bible is talking about when it says that God is a *jealous* God. He loves His people and wants them to turn away from sin and to love and worship Him. 2. To be angry and unhappy when someone else has something you want. The Bible calls this kind of *jealousy* a sin. 3. Being afraid of losing someone's love or affection.

Jehovah (je-HOV-ah)

This is an English translation of one of the Hebrew names for God. A more accurate name is Yahweh. This name was considered to be very holy.

Jerusalem (ju-ROO-sah-lem)

The most important city of Bible times. It was the capital of the united kingdom of Israel and, later, of the kingdom of Judah. The Temple was built in *Jerusalem*, so many people traveled to the city to worship God. In 587 B.C., *Jerusalem* was captured and mostly destroyed by Babylonian armies. The city was rebuilt when the Jews returned after 70 years of exile in Babylon. Jesus taught in *Jerusalem*, was crucified outside its wall, buried near it and then rose to life again. The first Christian church began in *Jerusalem* after the Holy Spirit came to the believers gathered there.

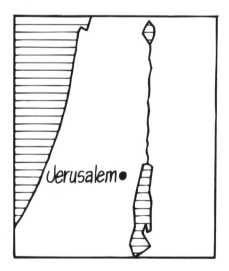

Jews (jooz)

At first, *Jews* referred to people who were members of the tribe of Judah. By New Testament times, however, *Jews* referred to people who were descendants of Abraham or who followed the Jewish religion (Judaism).

Judah (JOO-duh)

1. In Old Testament times, one of the sons of Jacob and Leah. 2. The descendants of *Judah*, who became the tribe of *Judah*. 3. The southern kingdom when the Israelites divided into two separate countries after the death of King Solomon. (The northern kingdom was called Israel.)

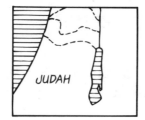

Judaism (JOO-day-izm)

The teachings of the Jewish religion. *Judaism* is based on worshiping the one true God, being circumcised as a sign of being one of God's chosen people, worshiping on the Sabbath (Saturday), obeying God's laws, and following other traditions given from one generation to another.

judge (juhj)

In the time of Moses, a *judge* helped people settle their disagreements. When the Israelites were settling the Promised Land after Joshua died, God chose leaders called *judges* to rule the people. Often these *judges* led the people in battle against their enemies. Deborah, Gideon and Samuel were *judges*. After kings began to rule Israel, *judges* once again settled disagreements and took care of official business.

judgment (JUHJ-munt)

1. In the Old Testament, *judgment* can mean God's laws or instructions. 2. *Judgment* can also mean God's punishment of a person or nation for disobeying Him. 3. In the New Testament, *judgment* can mean "to criticize or disapprove of someone." The Bible says Christians are not to pass *judgment* on each other. 4. *Judgment* can also mean the time of the end of the world as we know it, when God will *judge* sin and reward those people who have lived for Him.

justice (JUS-tiss)

That which is right and fair. Most of the prophets in the Bible emphasized that God is *just* and wants His people to act *justly*. Many of the warnings given by the prophets were because the leaders and people were guilty of *injustice*, or cheating others, especially poor people.

Justification (jus-tih-fih-KAY-shun)

God's action of treating sinners who have faith in Jesus Christ as if they had never sinned. God forgives their sin and becomes their friend. God also gives them the power to live in right ways. *Justification* is possible because Jesus Christ died to take the punishment for sin.

justify (JUS-tih-fy)

1. For God to erase someone's sin. 2. To announce that someone is right.

kingdom of heaven

The *kingdom of heaven* is also called the "kingdom of God." It means God's rule in the lives of His chosen people and His creation. In the Old Testament, the people in God's *kingdom* were the Israelites. In the New Testament and now, the people over whom God rules are Christians—people who love God and want to serve Him. A person becomes part of God's *kingdom* by trusting Jesus as his or her Savior and Lord. When

Jesus comes again, God's *kingdom* will become visible to all people.

kinsman

A relative.

Lamb of God

A name for Jesus that tells us that He died to take away our sins. When a Jewish person sinned, he or she offered a *lamb* as a sacrifice to God. Jesus became like one of those lambs when He gave Himself as a sacrifice to die so that our sins can be forgiven.

law

1. All the rules God gave to help people to know and love Him and to live happily with each other. The Ten Commandments are part of God's *law*. 2. A division of the Old Testament. The first five books of the Bible are called the books of the *Law*. 3. The entire Old Testament is sometimes called the *Law*. 4. Any rule that must be obeyed, whether it was decided by God or by people. 5. God's rules in the Old Testament plus other rules added by Jewish religious leaders. This is sometimes called the *Law*.

leprosy (LEP-ruh-see)

A name used for several serious skin diseases. People with *leprosy* were called *lepers*.

Jewish law said that *lepers* had to stay away from people who did not have the disease. *Lepers* lived outside their cities and towns, either by themselves or with other *lepers*, until the disease showed signs of healing.

Levites (LEE-vites)

Descendants of *Levi*, a son of Jacob and Leah. Some *Levites* were religious teachers. Others took care of the Tabernacle and, later, the Temple. Only *Levites* could become priests, but not all *Levites* were priests.

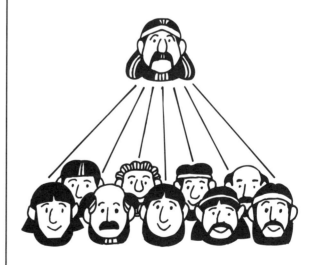

locusts (LOW-kusts)

A locust is a large insect like a grasshopper. Sometimes *locusts* travel in huge swarms, eating all the plants they can find. In Bible times, *locusts* were sometimes eaten as food.

lute (lute)

A stringed musical instrument with a pear-shaped body and a neck. It is played by plucking the strings.

lyre (lier)

A small harp with three to twelve strings. A *lyre* was held on the lap when it was played.

Magi (MAY-ji)

Men who lived in the countries of Arabia and Persia and who studied the stars. People thought the *Magi* had the power to tell the meaning of dreams. Several *Magi* followed a star to Bethlehem and brought Jesus expensive gifts to honor Him as a newborn king.

manger (MAIN-jur)

A box in a stable where food was placed for cattle, sheep, donkeys or other animals. When Jesus was born, His first bed was a *manger*.

manna (MAN-uh)

The special food God gave the Israelites for the 40 years they traveled in the desert. The Bible says that *manna* looked like white seeds or flakes and tasted sweet.

mantle (MAN-tul)

A loose-fitting outer robe or coat.

master (MAS-tur)

1. A name for Jesus. It means "teacher." 2. An overseer, boss, or owner of a slave.

mediator (MEE-dee-ay-tor)

A person who settles differences or arguments between two or more people. Jonathan was a *mediator* between David and Saul. Moses was a *mediator* between God and Israel. By paying the punishment for sin, Jesus became the *mediator* who makes it possible for us to have peace with God.

mercy

Showing more love or kindness to a person than he or she expects or deserves.

Messiah (mu-SIE-uh)

The Savior God promised to send. Jesus is the *Messiah*. In Hebrew, *Messiah* means "the Anointed One." In Greek, the word for "the Anointed One" is "Christos." "Christ" is the name used in the New Testament to show that Jesus is the *Messiah*.

millstone

One of a pair of large stones used to grind grain into flour.

miracle (MEER-uh-kul)

Some event or wonderful happening done by the power of God.

Moabite (MOE-uh-bite)

A person from the country of *Moab*, located just east of the Dead Sea. *Moab* often fought against Israel. At times it was under the control of Israel's kings.

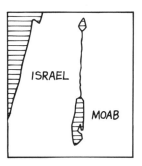

mortal (MOR-tuhl)

Able to die. All people, plants and animals are *mortal*. God is not *mortal*; He lives forever and will never die.

myrrh (murh)

The sap of the *myrrh* bush. *Myrrh* was used as a scent for anointing oil and perfume, as a pain killer, and to prepare a body for burial. The Magi brought Jesus a gift of *myrrh*.

nard

A pleasant-smelling oil made from the roots and stems of spikenard plant. This plant grew in India. Since the oil had to be brought from India to Israel, it was very expensive. Mary poured *nard* over Jesus' feet to show her love.

Nazarene (NAZ-uh-reen)

A person who lived in the town of Nazareth. Because Jesus lived in Nazareth for almost 30 years, He was often called a *Nazarene*. Later, Christians were sometimes called *Nazarenes* because they were followers of Jesus.

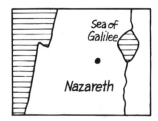

Nazirite (NAZ-uh-rite)

A Hebrew person who promised to serve God in a special way for a certain length of time. The time could be anywhere from 30 days to a lifetime. To show dedication to God, a *Nazirite* would not cut his or her hair, eat or drink anything made from grapes, or touch a dead body. At the end of the time, the person lived like other people. Samuel and Samson were *Nazirites* all their lives. Some scholars believe John the Baptist was also a *Nazirite*.

nomad (NO-mad)

A person who lives in a tent and moves from place to place. *Nomads* usually move when seasons change or when they need to find grass for feeding their animals. Abraham was a *nomad* for much of his life.

oath

A serious promise that what a person says is true. In Bible times, people often made an oath by saying "God is my witness." The oath often asked for God's punishment if what was said was not true. Jesus taught that people who love and obey Him do not need to make oaths because they should be known for saying only what is true.

offering (OFF-ring)

A gift of money, time or other possessions a person gives to God because he or she loves Him. In Old Testament times, people brought food and animals to the Tabernacle or Temple as *offerings* to God. The *offerings* were often burned on the altar. Animal *offerings* were always killed. Their blood symbolized sins being forgiven by death. Christians believe that we no longer need to *offer* sacrifices for the forgiveness of sins because Jesus' death is the once-for-all sacrifice through which our sins can be forgiven.

offspring

For humans, *offspring* are sons and daughters. For animals, *offspring* are their young.

oil

In the Bible, *oil* almost always means olive *oil*. *Oil* was squeezed from the olives and used in food, as a fuel for lamps, as a medicine for wounds, and as a hairdressing and skin softener. Olive *oil* was used to anoint priests and kings. It was also used in religious ceremonies in the Tabernacle and later in the Temple.

ordain (or-DANE)

1. To cause to happen. Psalm 65:9 says that the streams are filled with water to provide people with food because God has *ordained*—or caused—it. 2. To appoint or set apart a person to do special work. Paul was *ordained* to be a missionary to the Gentiles. 3. *Ordain* can also mean to decide or command.

overseer (OH-vur-seer)

A person who watches over and takes care of others. Joseph was an *overseer*; he watched over and directed other people who worked for Potiphar. In the New Testament, leaders in the Early Church were sometimes called *overseers*. Paul told these leaders to take care of the people in the church in the same way a good shepherd cares for his sheep.

ox, oxen

Strong male cattle. They were used for pulling plows, wagons and other heavy loads.

pagan (PAY-gun)

A person who does not worship the true God, especially a person who worships idols.

parable (PAIR-uh-bul)

A story that teaches a special lesson or truth. Jesus often told *parables* to teach important lessons.

paralytic (PAIR-uh-lih-tic)

A person who has lost the ability to move one or more arms and/or legs.

Passover

One of the Jews' most important feasts. The Jews celebrate *Passover* every spring as a reminder that God freed them from slavery in Egypt. The word *Passover* comes from the way the angel of death "passed over" the homes of Israelites on whose doorposts the blood of a lamb was sprinkled. In Egyptian homes, where there was no blood on the doorposts, all the firstborn sons died. This terrible disaster convinced the Egyptian Pharaoh to let the Israelites leave Egypt.

At the *Passover* feast, the Jews eat bread made without yeast (unleavened bread), bitter herbs and lamb. The unleavened bread reminds them that the Israelites left Egypt in a hurry. There was no time to let bread rise.

The bitter herbs remind them of their suffering in Egypt.

The lamb reminds them of the lamb they killed for the first *Passover*. The last meal Jesus ate with His disciples before He was crucified was a *Passover* feast.

Passover Lamb

The lamb killed at *Passover* as a sacrifice. The Bible says that Jesus is our *Passover Lamb*. He was sacrificed to deliver us from sin, just as the first *Passover Lamb* was sacrificed to deliver the firstborn sons of the Israelites from death and to provide them with escape from Egypt.

patriarch (PAY-tree-ark)

Either Abraham, Isaac or Jacob—the founders of the Hebrew nation. Jacob's (Israel's) 12 sons and King David are also called *patriarchs*.

Pentecost (PEN-te-cost)

A Jewish feast celebrated 50 days after Passover. Today the Christian church remembers *Pentecost* because on the first *Pentecost* after Jesus' resurrection, the Lord sent the Holy Spirit to His followers as He had promised. (See Acts 2.)

persecute (PUR-suh-cute)

To continually treat someone cruelly or unfairly, even though the person has done nothing wrong. The Early Christians were *persecuted* for teaching that Jesus is God's Son.

Pharaoh (FAY-row)

A title of the rulers of ancient Egypt, just as "president" or "king" or "prime minister" are titles of top officials in countries today.

Pharisee (FAIR-uh-see)

A Jew in the time of Jesus who tried very hard to obey every part of the Jewish law. Many sincerely tried to please God and to be holy. Some of the *Pharisees* worried more about keeping every little rule than about caring for people. Jesus often scolded the *Pharisees* because on the outside they seemed very holy, but on the inside, they were full of lies and hate (see Matthew 23). Saul of Tarsus (later called Paul) was a *Pharisee*.

plague (playg)

1. A very serious disease that spreads quickly among people in an area. It often causes death. 2. Anything that causes great harm or suffering. Crops may be destroyed by a *plague* of locusts. 3. The ten great disasters God sent to the Egyptians to convince Pharaoh to free the Israelites. Read about these *plagues* in Exodus 4—12.

plunder

1. To loot or rob, especially during a war. 2. The property taken by plundering. The gold Achan took was *plunder* that God had said not to take.

pomegranate (PAHM-uh-gran-ut)

A fruit about the size of an apple. The *pomegranate* fruit is encased in a tough, reddish skin. The fruit is ruby red, very juicy and filled with edible seeds. *Pomegranates* grow on small, bushy trees.

precepts (PREE-septs)

Commands, rules or laws.

predestined (pree-DEST-uhned)

Decided or chosen beforehand. In the Bible, the term refers to God's choice.

priest

1. A man among the Jews who offered prayers and sacrifices to God for the people. *Priests* led the public worship services at the Tabernacle, and later at the Temple. Often the *priests* also taught the Law of God to the people. The *priests* of Israel were all descendants of Aaron's family. 2. The New Testament says that Jesus Christ is now our *High Priest*, the One who offered Himself as the perfect sacrifice for our sins (see Hebrews 8,9). 3. All Christians are *priests* (see 1 Peter 2:9). We are to help others learn about and worship God.

proconsul (PRO-kon-sul)

A ruler in the Roman government. The Roman Empire was divided into provinces or states. The highest Roman official in each province was called the *proconsul*.

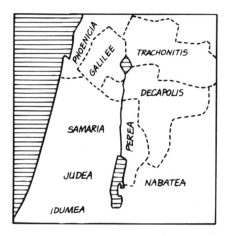

prophecy (PRAH-fuh-see)

The message from God that a *prophet* spoke or wrote to people. Some *prophecies* told about what God would do in the future.

prophets (PRAH-futs)

Men and women in the Old and New Testaments chosen by God to tell His messages to people.

prostitute (PRAH-sty-tute)

See *harlot*.

proverb (PRAH-verb)

A short, wise saying. The Bible book of *Proverbs* is made up of many wise sayings.

provoke (pruh-VOKE)

To make angry; to cause trouble on purpose.

psalm (salm)

A song or poem. A *psalm* usually praises God or tells the deep feelings of God's people. The Bible book of *Psalms* is made up of many Hebrew poems and songs.

purge (purj)

To make clean and pure.

Purim (POOR-im)

A Jewish holiday that celebrates the victory of Queen Esther and the Jews over wicked Haman.

rams

Mature male sheep. Rams were used for sacrifices and food. Their wool was used to make warm cloth and their horns were often used to make musical instruments called rams' horn trumpets.

ransom (RAN-sum)

1. The price paid to buy the freedom of a captive or slave. 2. In the New Testament, the price that Jesus paid to rescue all people (who are captives to sin and death) from the powers of sin and death.

raven (RAY-vun)

A large, black bird. Elijah was fed by *ravens*.

reap

To gather ripe grain and fruit. The Bible also uses the word *reap* to describe the reward or punishment people receive for their actions (see Galatians 6:9).

rebuke (ree-BUKE)

To correct someone sternly; to scold someone.

reconcile (REK-un-sile)

1. To help people who have been enemies become friends. 2. In the New Testament, bringing God and people together again through Jesus' life, death and resurrection. Sin separates people from God, but by dying, Jesus took the punishment for sin. When a person comes to know and love Jesus, he or she learns to love God instead of being His enemy. When this happens, the person is *reconciled* to God.

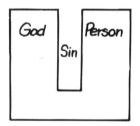

redeem (ree-DEEM)

1. To buy back. In Bible times, a person could pay a slave's owner whatever the slave was worth and then set the slave free. The slave had been *redeemed* by the person who had bought the slave and then set him or her free.

2. The New Testament tells us that by dying, Jesus *redeemed* us. He paid the price—His life—to buy us back and set us free from our slavery to sin.

reeds

Different plants growing in swamps or along the edges of water.

refuge (REF-uj)

A place where one is safe from danger; a shelter.

remnant (REM-nunt)

A small part that is left over. In the Old Testament, *remnant* usually refers to the few Israelite people who remained faithful worshipers of God after their exile in Babylon.

repent (ree-PENT)

To change one's mind; to turn around and go in the opposite direction. In the Bible, to *repent* means that you stop doing wrong action and start doing what God says is right. *Repentance* always involves making a change away from sin and toward God.

restore (ree-STORE)

1. To bring back; to establish again. 2. To bring back to a former or original condition. 3. To return something lost, stolen or taken.

resurrection (rez-ur-RECK-shun)

1. To come back to life after being dead. Jesus died and was buried; after three days, He rose from the dead. That event is called the *Resurrection*. It shows Jesus' power over sin and death. 2. A future time when everyone who has ever lived will live again in new, spiritual bodies that will never die. Those who do not love God will be separated from Him forever.

Jesus   Thomas

retribution (re-truh-BYOU-shun)

1. A payment that is deserved; revenge. 2. The punishment that comes to a person because he or she has broken God's law.

revelation (rev-uh-LAY-shun)

1. To make known something that was hidden or unknown. In Old Testament times, God *revealed* Himself through His mighty acts and through His words to the prophets and to other people, such as Abraham, Moses and David.

In the New Testament, God made Himself known by sending Jesus Christ. While Jesus lived on Earth, He revealed God's love, His holiness and His power. Jesus helps us know what God is like.

2. God's Word, the Bible. One of the ways God *reveals* Himself to us is through His Word. 3. The last book of the Bible is called the *Revelation* of Jesus Christ because it shows how Jesus will triumph over evil.

revenge (ree-VENGE)

Punishment, injury or harm done to pay back a wrong.

reverence (REV-er-unce)

A feeling of deep love and respect. *Reverence* should be our feeling about God and His holiness, power and love.

righteous (RYE-chuss)

1. God's character: God is *righteous* because He does only what is *right* and holy. 2. A person who has accepted Jesus as Savior. God sees that person as being free from the guilt of sin and sees the person as being *righteous*. 3. People who are members of God's family show their love for Him by living in *righteous* ways, thinking and doing what is *right* and holy.

Roman

1. A person who lived in the city of *Rome*. 2. A person who was a citizen of the *Roman* Empire. A *Roman* citizen enjoyed special rights and protection. For example, he or she could not be punished without a fair trial, nor could a *Roman* citizen be crucified.

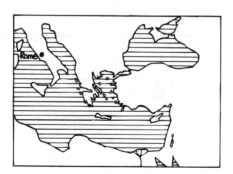

Sabbath (SAB-uth)

The weekly day of rest and worship God set apart for all people. In the Old Testament, it is the seventh day of the week (Saturday). For the Jew, *Sabbath* begins at sundown on Friday and lasts until sunset on Saturday.

Many Jews and some Christians observe the *Sabbath* on Saturday. Because Jesus rose from the dead on a Sunday, most Christians set aside Sunday as the day of rest and worship. (See Acts 20:7.)

sackcloth (SAK-kloth)

A rough, dark cloth usually woven from goats' hair. When someone died, the person's friends and family wore clothes made of *sackcloth* to show that they were very sad. A person would also wear *sackcloth* to show that he or she was sorry for sinning.

sacred (SAY-kred)

Holy; belonging to God.

sacrifice (SAK-rih-fice)

A gift or offering given to God. A *sacrifice* usually involved the killing of an animal to pay for sin. The New Testament tells us that Jesus died as the once-for-all *sacrifice* for sinners and that no further *sacrifices* for sin are necessary.

Sadducees (SAD-you-seez)

Jewish religious leaders in New Testament times. They said that only the laws in the first five books of the Old Testament had to be obeyed. They did not believe in the Resurrection or in angels or spirits. When the New Testament speaks of the "chief priests," it is referring to the *Sadducees*.

saints

The word means "God's people." The New Testament says that all Christians are saints. Paul often addressed his letters "to the saints."

salvation (sal-VAY-shun)

Sometimes *salvation* means to be rescued from evil. Sometimes it means to be kept from danger or death. In the New Testament, *salvation* usually means to be rescued from the guilt and power of sin. By His death and resurrection, Jesus brings *salvation* to people who believe in Him.

Samaritan (suh-MARE-uh-tun)

A person who lived in or came from the area in Israel known as *Samaria*. The *Samaritans* were only partly Jewish. They worshiped God differently than the other Jews. The Jews and *Samaritans* hated each other—perhaps because of the differences in the ways they worshiped. Jesus showed that He loved the *Samaritans* as much as any other people by traveling through *Samaria*, teaching the *Samaritans* about God. Jesus told the story of the *Good Samaritan*.

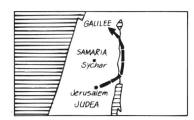

Most Jews traveled AROUND Samaria.

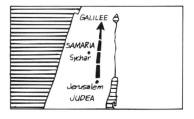

Jesus traveled THROUGH Samaria.

sanctify (SANK-tih-fie)

To set apart for God's use. When a person becomes a Christian, God says he or she is *sanctified*. Then the Holy Spirit continues helping him or her become more and more like Jesus, which is the process of *sanctification*.

sanctuary (SANK-choo-air-ee)

A holy place; a place where God is worshiped. In the Bible, *sanctuary* usually refers to the Tabernacle or to the Temple.

Tabernacle

Solomon's Temple

New Testament Temple

Sanhedrin (san-HEE-drun)

The highest Jewish political and religious court. In New Testament times, the *Sanhedrin* was made up of 70-100 men who were experts in Jewish laws. The *Sanhedrin* included the high priest, members of wealthy or prominent Jewish families, and members of the Pharisee and Sadducee religious groups.

Satan (SAY-tun)

The most powerful enemy of God and all people. Other names for *Satan* include: the devil; the evil one; the prince of this world; the father of lies. *Satan* is the ruler of a kingdom made up of demons. He hates God and tries to destroy God's work. The Bible tells us that in the end, God will destroy *Satan* and the demons.

Savior (SAVE-yur)

One who saves another. 1. The Old Testament almost always speaks of God as the *Savior* of His people. 2. Sometimes God sent someone to help His people, and that person was called a *savior*. 3. In the New Testament, *Savior* refers to Jesus. He died and rose again to rescue or *save* us from our sin.

scepter (SEP-tur)

A short rod held by a king or queen to show that he or she was the person with the most authority and power.

scorpion (SKOR-pee-un)

A large insect that is a member of the spider family. It has a long tail with a poisonous stinger on the end. Its sting can kill a small animal and is very painful to humans.

scribe

1. An expert in understanding the Jewish law. *Scribes* taught the people God's laws. They also copied the Old Testament writings onto scrolls. Ezra was a *scribe*. By New Testament times, the *scribes* often served as judges in Jewish courts because they knew so much about the law. 2. A writer or secretary who earned his living writing letters or important papers for other people.

Scripture (SKRIP-chur)

The Bible. The word *Scripture* means "writing." Before the New Testament was written down, *Scripture* meant the Old Testament. After the New Testament was written down, Christians began calling both the Old and New Testaments *Scripture*.

scroll (skrole)

A long strip of papyrus or parchment with writing on it. A stick was attached at each end of the strip so that it could be rolled up to make it easier to read, store and carry.

seal

Also called a signet. A small tool or ring that had a design cut into one side. The owner of each seal had his or her own special design. When the owner wanted to put his or her own special mark or brand on something, the person would press the *seal* into hot wax or soft clay. As the wax or clay hardened, it kept the design in it. *Seals* were used to show that two people had reached an agreement, to seal a letter and to show who owned something.

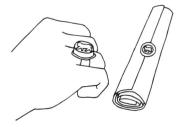

seer (SEE-uhr)

A prophet; a person who, with God's help, could see what would happen in the future.

sensual (SEN-shoo-uhl)

1. Appealing to the body's senses. 2. Caring too much for physical pleasures.

servant

A person who works for the comfort or protection of others. Jesus said that He is a *servant*. He instructed His followers to be *servants* to each other instead of trying to have authority over each other. In the Bible, the word *servant* sometimes means slave.

sexual immorality

To use sex in ways that God says are wrong. Sexual union between two people who are not married to each other is a sin.

sheaf, sheaves (sheef, sheevz)

A bundle or bundles of cut grain stalks.

sheep pen or **sheepfold**

A protected place for sheep to stay.

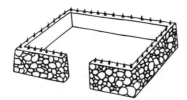

shekel (SHEK-uhl)

A small weight of silver or gold (usually a small ball of metal) that was used as money.

shepherd (SHEP-urd)

A person who takes care of sheep. A shepherd finds grass and water for the sheep, protects them from bad weather and wild animals, brings them safely into a sheepfold at night, and cares for sick or hurt sheep.

sickle

A tool with a sharp curved blade that is attached to a short handle. A *sickle* is used to cut stalks of grain.

siege (seej)

Surrounding a city or town with an army so that no one or nothing can go in or out. The purpose of a *siege* is to make the city or town surrender.

signet

See *seal*.

sin

Any act or thought that is against the way God wants us to act or think. The Bible says that all people have *sinned*. *Sin* separates us from God. God sent Jesus to die to take the punishment for *sin*. Because Jesus died, our *sins* can be forgiven and the separation between God and us can be removed.

I have done wrong. Forgive me.

slander

To say untrue things about a person in order to hurt his or her reputation. The Bible says that *slander* is a sin.

slave

A servant who is owned by his or her master and could be bought or sold like property. People became *slaves* if they were defeated in battle by an enemy or if they were unable to pay their debts. A *slave* had to do whatever the master ordered.

Son of Man

A name for Jesus. Jesus called Himself the *Son of Man* many times. The name means that Jesus is a real man and that He is the One God promised to send in Daniel 7:13.

soothsayer (SOOTH-say-er)

A person who said he or she could tell what would happen in the future—a fortune-teller. Both the Old and New Testaments say that *soothsaying* is wrong.

sorcerer (SORE-sir-er)

A person who claimed to be able to make evil spirits work for him or her. The Bible says that *sorcery* is a sin.

soul

In the Bible, the word *soul* usually refers to the part of a person that cannot be seen but that controls what a person thinks, feels and does. Sometimes *soul* means the whole living person. The words *soul* and "spirit" usually mean about the same thing.

sovereign (SOV-run)

Having authority and power over everything. God is *sovereign*.

sow

To plant seeds. In Bible times, a farmer *sowed* seeds by scattering them by hand over a plowed field.

spirit

The unseen part of a person that controls what he or she thinks, feels and does; soul. The Bible says that God is a *spirit.* He does not have a physical body.

staff

1. A strong stick used for support when walking or climbing. 2. A strong wooden rod with a hook on the end used by a shepherd as he cared for sheep.

statute (STAT-chewt)

A law or command. In the Bible, *statute* usually refers to God's law.

stiff-necked

Stubborn, rebellious and unwilling to learn.

stone

To throw large stones and rocks at a person until he or she is dead. *Stoning* was the way people were punished for disobeying certain parts of the Jewish law. Stephen was *stoned* for teaching that Jesus is God's Son. (See Acts 7.)

submission

To choose to work with or to obey another person in a thoughtful, gentle way. The Bible says that Christians are to *submit* to each other in the same way Jesus *submitted* to God when He lived on Earth.

synagogue (SIN-uh-gog)

A place where Jews meet together to read and study the Old Testament and to worship God.

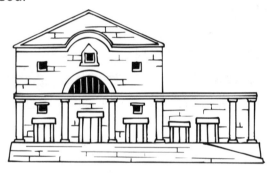

Tabernacle (TAB-er-nack-ul)

The portable tent where the Israelites worshiped God. They used it while they wandered in the desert after they left Egypt and for many years after they entered the Promised Land. Moses and the people built the *Tabernacle* following God's instructions. The *Tabernacle* was used until it was replaced by a permanent place of worship called the Temple. The *Tabernacle* is described in detail in Exodus 26.

talent

A large amount of silver or gold worth a huge amount of money. One *talent* was considered to be the amount of money a worker would earn in about 10 years.

Temple (TEM-pul)

The permanent place in Jerusalem where the Jews worshiped God. The first *Temple* was built by King Solomon and the people, following the building instructions God had given Solomon's father, King David. The *Temple* was a very beautiful place. It was destroyed and rebuilt twice. In A.D. 64, the *Temple* was destroyed again. It has not been rebuilt.

Solomon's Temple
(See 1 Kings 6—8.)

Second Temple
(See Ezra and Nehemiah.)

Herod's Temple
(See Matthew—Acts.)

tempt

1. To test a person to improve his or her spiritual strength. 2. To try to get someone to do something wrong.

testimony (TEST-ih-moan-ee)

1. In the Old Testament, *testimony* often refers to the Law of God. 2. In the New Testament, *testimony* usually means giving proof that something is true.

tetrarch (TET-rarck)

When a country in the Roman Empire was divided into sections, the ruler of each part was called a *tetrarch*. In the New Testament, Herod Antipas is sometimes called a *tetrarch* and sometimes a king. He was the ruler of Galilee in the time of Jesus.

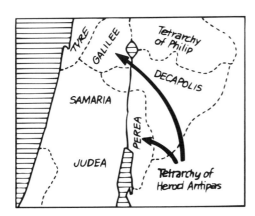

threshing floor

The place where grain was trampled by oxen or beaten with a stick to separate the heads of grain from the stalk. A *threshing floor* was usually a large, flat rock or a large area of clay that was packed hard. *Threshing floors* were usually built where wind would blow away the chaff and leave the heavier grain.

tithe

To give God one-tenth of what you earn. For example, if you had 10 dimes, you would *tithe* by giving 1 dime to God.

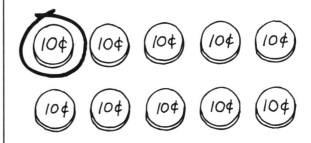

tomb (tume)

A place where dead people are buried. In Bible times, tombs were often natural caves or rooms dug into stone cliffs. Large stones were placed over the entrances to these tombs to close them.

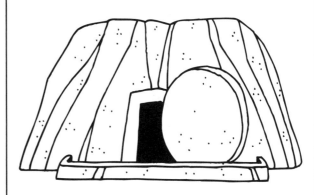

trance (trans)

In the Bible, a *trance* means a deep, dream-like state in which a person received a message from God. Peter was in a *trance* when God showed him the vision of the animals in a sheet (see Acts 10:10).

transfigured (tranz-FIG-yurd)

To have been changed in appearance or form. The Bible tells us that Jesus' physical appearance was changed—*transfigured*—as three of His disciples watched. His face glowed and His clothes became shining white. Moses and Elijah appeared and Jesus talked with them about His coming death.

This is my Son, whom I love.

transgression (trans-GRESH-un)

A sin; disobeying the law of God.

treaty (TREE-tee)

A formal agreement between people, groups or countries.

trespass (TRES-pass)

To go against the rights of someone else. We *trespass* against people when we do something unfair to them or when we break laws made to protect people. We *trespass* against God when we break His laws. In the Bible, another word for *trespass* is "sin."

I didn't take it.

tribute (TRIB-yoot)

In the Bible, *tribute* usually means money or services that a weaker nation had to pay to a stronger nation.

trumpet

A straight tube with a mouthpiece at one end and a bell-shaped flare at the other. *Trumpets* were played at every Temple service.

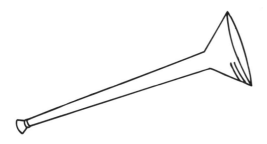

trumpet of rams' horns

A curved ram's horn, blown as a signal. *Trumpets of rams' horns* were used in religious ceremonies and in battle.

tunic (TOO-nik)

A loose shirt reaching to the knees. A *tunic* was usually worn as an undergarment.

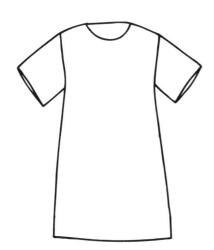

turban (TER-bun)

A head covering made by twisting cloth and wrapping it around the head.

unclean

Unclean does not just mean dirty. It also means any action, thought, food, person or place that God had said is displeasing to Him. One of the ways a Jewish person could become *unclean* was by eating food God had said not to eat. Other ways a person could become *unclean* were by touching a dead body or by getting a skin disease called leprosy. A person could become clean again by going through certain ceremonies.

unleavened bread (un-LEV-und)

Bread made without yeast. *Unleavened bread* is usually flat, like a pancake or cracker.

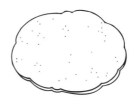

vengeance (VEN-juhns)

Punishment for wrongdoing. In the Old Testament, a person was told exactly how much he or she could do to punish someone for a wrong he or she had done. But the New Testament tells people not to punish those who have wronged them. Instead, they are told to trust God to take care of the punishment, because He is the only one who is completely fair and just.

vile

Disgusting or evil.

violate (VIE-oh-late)

1. To break the law. 2. To force someone to have sex; to rape. 3. To make something unholy.

viper (VIE-pur)

A poisonous snake.

virgin (VIR-gin)

A person who has never had sexual intercourse.

vision (VIH-zuhn)

A *vision* was a way God showed someone a truth that would otherwise not be known. God used *visions* to show a message of truth in pictures. Sometimes, people were asleep when God gave them *visions* (see Ezekiel 8:1-4 and Acts 10:9-29).

vow

A promise made to God.

wail

A long, loud cry to show sorrow.

widow

A woman whose husband has died.

wilderness (WILL-der-ness)

A large area of land where few people live. Depending on the amount of rainfall, the land might be a barren desert or it might grow grass and other vegetation on which sheep and other herds of animals could graze.

wineskin

A bag made from an animal skin. Wine, milk, water and grape juice were stored in *wineskins*.

winnow (WIN-oh)

To separate the kernels of grain from the worthless husks. Once the husks were loosened from the grain, the grain was tossed into the air when there was a strong breeze. The breeze would blow away the light husks and the heavier kernels of grain would fall to the ground.

witness

1. A person who tells what he or she has seen. Jesus told His followers to be witnesses. 2. To tell others what you have seen. We are to tell (or witness to) what we have seen Jesus Christ do in our own lives.

woe

Misery, sorrow or great suffering.

womb (woom)

The part of a woman's body where a baby grows until it is born.

wonder

A miracle; a thing or event that causes surprise and awe. God did many wonders to convince Pharaoh to let the Israelites leave Egypt.

world

1. The planet Earth. 2. People who follow Satan. 3. Anything that belongs to life on Earth instead of eternal life with God.

worldly

Being part of life on Earth instead of eternal life with God. The Bible warns against loving the things of the world more than the things of God.

worship (WUR-ship)

Anything a person does to show love and respect. Some people *worship* idols. Some people *worship* the one true God.

wrath (rath)

Very great anger.

Yahweh

An English equivalent of the Hebrew word for God; also translated "Jehovah."

yoke

1. A wooden bar that goes over the necks of two animals, usually oxen. The *yoke* holds the animals together when they are pulling something such as a cart or plow. 2. Two oxen *yoked* together.

3. *Yoke* is sometimes used as a word picture for any burden or demand. Slavery, imprisonment, taxes or unfair laws were called *yokes*.

4. A partnership.

Zealot (Zel-ut)

A member of a Jewish group in the time of Jesus that wanted to fight against and overthrow the Roman rulers in Israel. Jesus' disciple Simon (not the same man as Simon Peter) was a *Zealot*.

Zion (Zie-un)

1. One of the hills upon which the city of Jerusalem was built; Mount *Zion*.

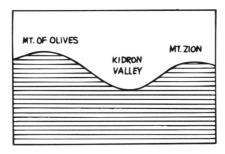

2. The entire city of Jerusalem; the city of *Zion*.

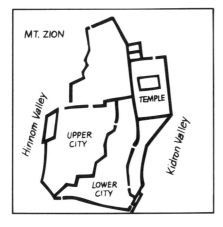

3. Another name for the nation of Israel; the people of *Zion*.

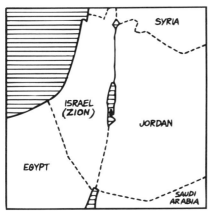

4. Another name for Heaven.

BIBLE DICTIONARY
Dot Definitions

Connect the dots to find four words (each "1" begins a new letter). Use a Bible dictionary to find the definition of each word, and then draw lines to match each word with its definition. (Watch out for the extra definition!)

An agreement between God and His people.

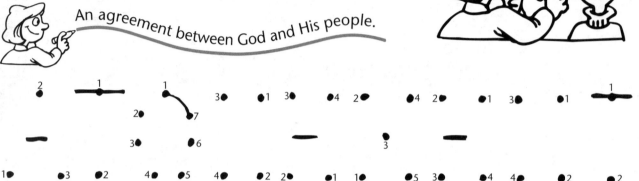

To buy back. Jesus paid the price to "buy us back" and set us free from our slavery to sin.

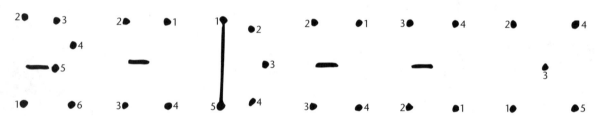

To make someone angry on purpose.

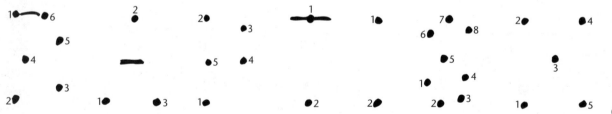

To make up for a wrong act. Jesus did this by dying on the cross for our sins.

Using water to show that someone is a member of God's family.

BIBLE DICTIONARY
WORD WORKS

Use a Bible dictionary to help you circle the correct definition for each of the words below.

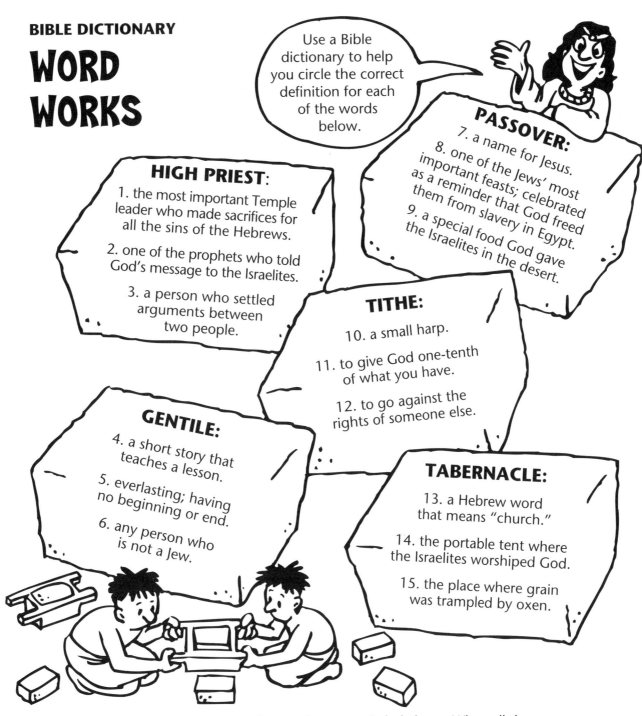

HIGH PRIEST:

1. the most important Temple leader who made sacrifices for all the sins of the Hebrews.

2. one of the prophets who told God's message to the Israelites.

3. a person who settled arguments between two people.

PASSOVER:

7. a name for Jesus.

8. one of the Jews' most important feasts; celebrated as a reminder that God freed them from slavery in Egypt.

9. a special food God gave the Israelites in the desert.

TITHE:

10. a small harp.

11. to give God one-tenth of what you have.

12. to go against the rights of someone else.

GENTILE:

4. a short story that teaches a lesson.

5. everlasting; having no beginning or end.

6. any person who is not a Jew.

TABERNACLE:

13. a Hebrew word that means "church."

14. the portable tent where the Israelites worshiped God.

15. the place where grain was trampled by oxen.

Now color in the squares containing the numbers you circled above. When all the squares are correctly colored in, you will find the word that means to tell God or others about your sins.

1	1	1	2	1	1	1	2	1	2	3	2	1	3	1	1	1	3	1	1	1	2	1	1	1	2	1	1	1
6	5	5	4	6	4	6	4	6	6	5	5	6	4	6	4	4	5	6	4	5	5	6	4	5	4	6	4	4
8	7	9	7	8	9	8	7	8	9	8	7	8	9	8	8	8	7	8	8	8	9	8	8	8	7	8	8	8
11	12	10	12	11	10	11	10	11	12	12	11	11	10	11	12	10	12	11	12	10	10	10	12	11	10	12	10	11
14	14	14	15	14	14	14	15	14	13	13	13	14	15	14	13	13	15	14	14	14	14	13	14	14	14	15	14	14	14

BIBLE WORD DEFINITIONS
Code Fill in

A = __ books in the Old Testament
D = __ books in the Gospels
E = __ followers sent by Jesus
    to tell about Him
    (Luke 9:1,2)
H = __ gifts of the wise men
    (Matthew 2:11)
J = __ books in the New
    Testament
M = __ books in the Bible
P = __ chapters in Genesis
R = __ chapters in Acts
S = __ chapters in Revelation
U = __ verses in the Bible's longest chapter
    (Psalm 119)
V = __ days it rained while Noah was in the ark (Genesis 7:12)
W = __ years Joseph lived (Genesis 50:22)

Use your Bible to fill in the missing numbers. Then use the code to discover two very important words.

$\underset{39}{\_}\ \underset{50}{\_}\ \underset{22}{O}\ \underset{22}{\_}\ \underset{}{T}\ \underset{}{L}\ \underset{12}{\_}\ =\ \underset{39}{\_}\ \underset{50}{\_}\ \underset{12}{\_}\ \underset{28}{\_}\ \underset{22}{\_}\ \underset{}{O}\ \underset{}{N}$

O T L = O N
39 50 22 12 39   50 12 28 22

N T O T
22 12   176   39 22   39

N G
66 12 22 22 12   12 28 .

I T N = T O T L L
110   12 22 22   12

O T T Y O
  3 12 28 22   110 3 39   176

N.
3 39 40 12   22 12 12

T O T L
  3 12   39 50 22   12 22

I T N B O T
110   12 22 22 12 4   39   176

.
27 12 22 176 22

216

© 2005 Gospel Light. Permission to photocopy granted. *The Big Book of Bible Facts and Fun*

BIBLE WORD DEFINITIONS
Ferris Wheel Definitions

__ __ __ __ __ __ __ __ : a man or woman

__ __ __ __ __ __ __ __ __ __ __ __ __ __

to __ __ __ __ __ or __ __ __ __ __ God's

message (__ __ __ __ __ __ __ __) to others.

__ __ __ __ __ __ __ __ __ __ __ __ : to

__ __ __ __ __ __ __ __ __ __ something that was

__ __ __ __ __ __ or __ __ __ __ __ __ __ .

(__ __ __ shows what He is like

through His actions and the

world He made.)

Bonus: Read Jonah 3:8,9 to find out what one prophet said.

Begin at the arrow and write every other letter in order on the blank lines. Cross off the letters on the Ferris wheel as you move around it. Keep going until the puzzle is complete. You will find the definitions of two words that help us understand more about God's messages.

BIBLE DICTIONARY
Dot Definitions

Connect the dots to find four words (each "1" begins a new letter). Use a Bible dictionary to find the definition of each word, and then draw lines to match each word with its definition. (Watch out for the extra definition!)

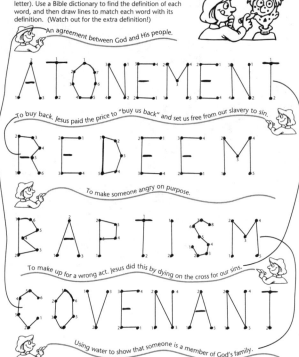

An agreement between God and His people.

ATONEMENT

To buy back. Jesus paid the price to "buy us back" and set us free from our slavery to sin.

REDEEM

To make someone angry on purpose.

BAPTISM

To make up for a wrong act. Jesus did this by dying on the cross for our sins.

COVENANT

Using water to show that someone is a member of God's family.

BIBLE DICTIONARY
WORD WORKS

Use a Bible dictionary to help you circle the correct definition for each of the words below.

HIGH PRIEST:
1. the most important Temple leader who made sacrifices for all the sins of the Hebrews.
2. one of the prophets who told God's message to the Israelites.
3. a person who settled arguments between two people.

PASSOVER:
7. a name for Jesus.
8. one of the Jews' most important feasts; celebrated as a reminder that God freed them from slavery in Egypt.
9. a special food God gave the Israelites in the desert.

TITHE:
10. a small harp.
11. to give God one-tenth of what you have.
12. to go against the rights of someone else.

GENTILE:
4. a short story that teaches a lesson.
5. everlasting; having no beginning or end.
6. any person who is not a Jew.

TABERNACLE:
13. a Hebrew word that means "church."
14. the portable tent where the Israelites worshiped God.
15. the place where grain was trampled by oxen.

Now color in the squares containing the numbers you circled above. When all the squares are correctly colored in, you will find the word that means to tell God or others about your sins.

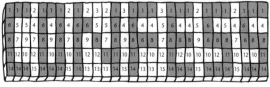

BIBLE WORD DEFINITIONS
Code Fill In

A = **39** books in the Old Testament
D = **4** books in the Gospels
E = **12** followers sent by Jesus to tell about Him (Luke 9:1,2)
H = **3** gifts of the wise men (Matthew 2:11)
J = **27** books in the New Testament
M = **66** books in the Bible
P = **50** chapters in Genesis
R = **28** chapters in Acts
S = **22** chapters in Revelation
U = **176** verses in the Bible's longest chapter (Psalm 119)
V = **40** days it rained while Noah was in the ark (Genesis 7:12)
W = **110** years Joseph lived (Genesis 50:22)

Use your Bible to fill in the missing numbers. Then use the code to discover two very important words.

```
A P O S T L E = A  P E R S O N
39 50 22 12 176 12  39  50 12 28 22

S E N T  O U T  A S  A
22 12  176  39 22  39

M E S S E N G E R.
66 12 22 22 12 12 28

W I T N E S S = T O  T E L L
110  12 22 22  12  12

O T H E R S  W H A T  Y O U
12  28 39  12  110 3 39   176

H A V E  S E E N.
3 39 40 12  22 12 12

T H E  A P O S T L E S
3 12  39 50 22  12 22

W I T N E S S E D  A B O U T
110  12 22 12 4  39  176

J E S U S.
27 12 22 176 22
```

BIBLE WORD DEFINITIONS
Ferris Wheel Definitions

Prophet: a man or woman **chosen by God** to **write** or **speak** God's message (**prophecy**) to others.

Revelation: to **make known** something that was **hidden** or **unknown**.

(**God** shows what He is like through His actions and the world He made.)

Begin at the arrow and write every other letter in order on the blank lines. Cross off the letters on the Ferris wheel as you move around it. Keep going until the puzzle is complete. You will find the definitions of two words that help us understand more about God's messages.

Bonus: Read Jonah 3:8,9 to find out what one prophet said.

BIBLE CHARACTER INDEX

Honor Your
Sunday School Teachers

**On Sunday School Teacher Appreciation Day
the Third Sunday in October**

Churches across America are invited to set aside the third Sunday in October as a day to honor Sunday School teachers for their dedication, hard work and life-changing impact on their students. That's why Gospel Light launched **Sunday School Teacher Appreciation Day** in 1993, with the goal of honoring the 15 million Sunday School teachers nationwide who dedicate themselves to teaching the Word of God to children, youth and adults.

Visit **www.mysundayschoolteacher.com** to learn great ways to honor your teachers on Sunday School Teacher Appreciation Day and throughout the year.

NOMINATE YOUR TEACHERS
FOR SUNDAY SCHOOL TEACHER
OF THE YEAR!
**Winner Receives a Dream Vacation
to Hawaii!**

An integral part of Sunday School Teacher Appreciation Day is the national search for the **Sunday School Teacher of the Year.** This award was established in honor of Dr. Henrietta Mears— a famous Christian educator who influenced the lives of such well-known and respected Christian leaders as Dr. Billy Graham, Bill and Vonette Bright, Dr. Richard Halverson and many more.

You can honor your Sunday School teachers by nominating them for this award. If one of your teachers is selected, he or she will receive **a dream vacation for two to Hawaii,** plus free curriculum, resources and more for your church!

Nominate your teachers online at **www.mysundayschoolteacher.com** or call the Sunday School Teacher Appreciation Day hotline—**1-800-354-4224**—to receive more information.

Sponsored by

Gospel Light

*Helping you honor Sunday School teachers,
the unsung heroes of the faith.*

Partners

More Great Resources from Gospel Light

The Big Book of Bible Story Art Activities for Ages 3 to 6
Young children will love hearing favorite Bible stories as they enjoy creative art activities. Instructions for making puppets, collages, chalk art, friendship bracelets and more are provided to help children create Bible story art. Reproducible, perforated pages.
ISBN 08307.33086

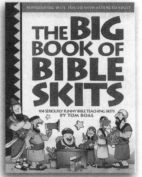

The Big Book of Bible Skits
Tom Boal

104 seriously funny Bible-teaching skits. Each skit comes with Bible background, performance tips, prop suggestions, discussion questions and more. Ages 10 to adult. Reproducible.
ISBN 08307.19164

The Really Big Book of Kids' Sermons and Object Talks with CD-ROM
This reproducible resource for children's pastors is packed with 156 sermons (one a week for three years) that are organized by topics such as friendship, prayer, salvation and more. Each sermon includes an object talk using a household object, discussion questions, prayer and optional information for older children. Reproducible.
ISBN 08307.36573

The Big Book of Volunteer Appreciation Ideas
Joyce Tepfer

This reproducible book is packed with 100 great thank-you ideas for teachers, volunteers and helpers in any children's ministry program. An invaluable resource for showing your gratitude!
ISBN 08307.33094

The Big Book of Christian Growth
Discipling made easy! 306 discussion cards based on Bible passages, and 75 games and activities for preteens. Reproducible.
ISBN 08307.25865

The Big Book of Bible Skills
Active games that teach a variety of Bible skills (book order, major divisions of the Bible, location references, key themes). Ages 8 to 12. Reproducible.
ISBN 08307.23463

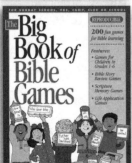

The Big Book of Bible Games
200 fun, active games to review Bible stories and verses and to apply Bible truths to everyday life. For ages 6 to 12. Reproducible.
ISBN 08307.18214

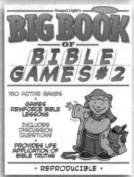

The Big Book of Bible Games #2
150 active games—balloon games, creative team relays, human bowling, and more—that combine physical activity with Bible learning. Games are arranged by Bible theme and include discussion questions. For grades 1 to 6. Reproducible.
ISBN 08307.30532

To order, visit your local Christian bookstore or www.gospellight.com

Gospel Light
God's Word for a Kid's World!™

Smart Resources for Your Children's Ministry

Children's Ministry is quickly becoming the Church's top priority. The urgency of reaching children for Christ before age 13 has resulted in an abundance of ministry ideas and opportunities. It's an exciting time for children's pastors and teachers and they are busier than ever!

That's why Gospel Light's *Smart Pages* are the perfect resource for people involved in children's ministry. They help leaders evaluate the purpose and goals of their programming, and then help them develop the practical elements for realizing their ministry goals. Tested by teachers and leaders, the information in these comprehensive resources has been proven to work in real-life children's ministries.

NEW! Children's Ministry Smart Pages with CD-ROM

This comprehensive guide provides you with all the information you need to create an effective children's ministry. Reproducible.

This book also includes—
- Miniposters that highlight key teaching skills
- A CD-ROM containing everything that's in the book

ISBN 08307.30966

NEW! Preteen Ministry Smart Pages

Gordon and Becki West

Gordon and Becki West offer a solid, practical and comprehensive understanding of how to build an effective ministry that reaches this vital age group. Covers such topics as understanding preteens, making preteen youth groups work, motivating and nurturing preteens, ministering to the families of preteens, and recruiting and managing ministry volunteers.

Anyone who has a heart for helping kids make the difficult transition from childhood to adolescence will find a wealth of information and ideas in this rich and much-needed resource.

ISBN 08307.37111

Early Childhood Smart Pages

Sheryl Haystead

Complete resource for planning and organizing an effective ministry to young children, plus articles on key topics of interest for teachers. Reproducible.

ISBN 08307.29321

Sunday School Smart Pages

Advice, answers and articles on teaching children ages 2 to 12. Reproducible.

ISBN 08307.15215

Nursery Smart Pages

How to begin or maintain a quality nursery ministry. Includes safety guidelines, complete recruitment helps, teacher training, clip art and more! Reproducible.

ISBN 08307.19067

Gospel Light
God's Word for a Kid's World!™

To order, visit your local Christian bookstore or www.gospellight.com

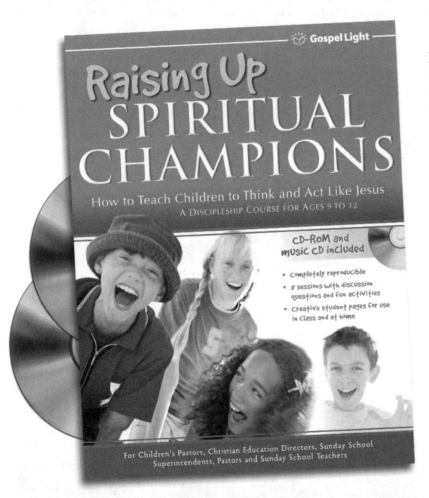